Two plays
Fuente Ovejuna
Lost in a Mirror

Fuente Ovejuna

Lost in a Mirror
(It Serves Them Right)

Two plays by
Lope de Vega

In new versions by
Adrian Mitchell

Introduction by
Nicholas Dromgoole

absolute classics

These translations were first published in 1989 by Absolute Press.

Reprinted August 1990

Produced and printed in England by
The Longdunn Press Ltd, Bristol
Cover illustration by Lo Cole.

ISBN 0 948230 23 1

Contents

Introduction

In spite of all the evidence still available, the clothes, the artefacts, the buildings, the pictures, whole libraries of books and written material, the attitudes and assumptions underpinning seventeenth century working lives, still seem extraordinarily elusive. What did they really think and feel? Even in his most intimate moments, confiding his scabrous thoughts in code to his intensely personal and private diary, Samuel Pepys speaks to us across a distance of centuries, and we are uneasily aware that although we share the same words, all too often they meant quite different things then from now. Even with 'table and chair', there are serious stylistic differences and wildly different visual judgements, but what about words like "honour", "hero", "reputation"?

If we can find ourselves bogged down in incomprehension even in our own English history, across such a relatively short time span, then it is doubly difficult for the English reader to come to terms with Spanish literature. It is not so much that we see a play by Lope de Vega in a quite different kind of theatre from his, nor that it comes to us filtered through a translation which, however painstaking, sensitive and well written, interposes yet another barrier between the playwright and ourselves. It is more that the play was written for a particular kind of audience, sharing sets of commonly agreed values, a cultural view of the world, a weltanschaung, different even then in crucial areas from an English audience's, but one which now seems foreign to us in every sense. We are not the kind of audience for which these plays were written. If the plays still succeeed in the theatre, and they do, it is often in spite of, rather than because of the author's intentions; often just because they happen to chime in with our pre-occupations, however different from the author's, so that we decode these signals from a distant era, all too often in terms of what is significant for us, sometimes blithely oblivious of what they originally conveyed. A modern audience responds to Shakespeare's "Romeo and Juliet" in terms of romantic love, part and parcel of the Romantic Movement, and now almost a cliché of popular films, novels, serials in women's magazines and a staple of television fiction. [If you think I should be writing about Lope de Vega and not Shakespeare, bear with me. They were contemporaries, and it is sometimes easier to move from the known to the unknown.] Shakespeare's audience knew nothing of our romantic attitudes, but doubtless remembered with secret and acute embarrassment the fools that they made of themselves in early adolescence, when they first fell in love. Shakespeare was reminding them, not of the clumsy, cringe-making ways they actually behaved, but of how their calf-love had seemed at the time, as devastating as a thunderclap from heaven, a vision of poetry and finer feeling in a mundane world. In their society of arranged marriages, where women were so strictly controlled they could not even act on stage the equality between the sexes that Shakespeare was radically championing, where Juliet herself had to be played by a boy, the Elizabethan response, the understanding they brought to the performance, must have been wildy different from our own.

Yet the play still works, and surely this is what matters, even if the negotiation between text and audience, between signifier and signified, is now profoundly different. Living theatre is about here and now; that mysterious moment when the curtain rises and conversation stills into a hush of expectancy from an audience that has paid for the privilege of being entertained, in that peculiarly vivid magic which only live actors in direct communication with a responsive audience can create.

When the drama historian raises a shrill voice, gnashing his aged and ill-fitting teeth, and brandishing his categories like an unwanted Polonius, to tell us we have got it all wrong, who really cares?

Perhaps, at heart, we all do. Once the play has succeeded in our terms, in our imaginative world, it has established its fascination for us, and we are naturally curious about it. When we gossip about our friends, it is not just love of gossip as such, but love of our friends too, that motivates us. They fascinate us and we want to know as much as possible about them. It is the same with plays and playwrights. We have that nagging desire to know. Are we missing something? So that the more we know about the context of the play, the social milieu for which it was written, the kind of theatre in which it appeared, what clues there are to the author's original intentions, what he thought he was saying, and how his original audience might have reacted, the more we can add to the impact of the play on ourselves as twentieth century playgoers. Because part of the burden of coming at the end of a long and remarkably rich theatre tradition, is we simply have to be knowledgeable about that tradition if we are fully to benefit from it.

It was probably always thus. Five centuries before the birth of Christ, Athenians at the theatre must have prided themselves on coming at the end of a long and noble theatre tradition. Elizabethan audiences probably lamented the demise of the mystery plays, so carefully and opulently organised by the church only a generation earlier, and intellectuals probably sounded all too recognisably superior as they drew parallels and recognised influences. But it has only been with the arrival of the Romantic Movement, that Europeans grew so obsessed with the past, wallowed in nostalgia, became historically conscious, and systematically and sympathetically studied previous centuries. Only in the nineteenth century, as part of that romanticism, were plays consciously presented in sets and costumes which attempted to be historically accurate. Shakespeare's and Lope de Vega's plays were presented in modern dress.

So perhaps we should look first at the kind of theatre Lope de Vega was writing for. It was a popular theatre. Historians of English drama tend to see the rise of English Renaissance theatre, a commercial popular theatre, as being forced on us by the weakness and impoverishment of the Church after Henry VIII, so that where Church and Guilds between them had organised theatre, as their influence waned, commercialism and free enterprise touring companies stepped in to fill the vacuum and take advantage of the nationwide enthusiasm for drama already created. Events in Spain should teach us to approach this simplification with caution. While helpful enough as generalisation, it ignores too many factors in a complex situation. The Church continued throughout Spain's golden age of theatre from 1492 to 1700, to organise and present drama as it had done in the Middle Ages. Yet independent touring companies and theatres built specially to house them grew up alongside the Church theatre. In fact throughout Europe, and including England, a sub-culture of touring theatre companies had existed from the days of the Roman empire, and seems to have survived throughout the Dark Ages and certainly flourished throughout the Middle Ages. Because of language and dialect problems, this theatre, the theatre of fairs and feast days, was a highly accomplished mime theatre, a theatre of gesture rather than words. In the absence of scripts, written evidence about it is scanty, but quite enough to put its continued existence beyond doubt. With the emergence of common national languages in the sixteenth and seventeenth centuries, a new kind of verbal theatre developed alongside and gradually superseded the mime theatre. It is worth remembering that the play within the play in Hamlet starts, as plays usually did, with an account in mime of the plot. Even in Shakespeare's day audience's "read" mime gestures much more easily than understanding the words. When a modern audience "reads" the programme note in order to understand a ballet at Covent Garden they are doing the exact opposite. Nothing could better illustrate just how far removed we are from those audiences of Lope de Vega and Shakespeare. [One reason why the actors seem not to have required directors was that they and the audience shared a common visual language of gesture, a centuries old European tradition that everyone so took for granted it was hardly ever mentioned.]

The difference in these developments between England and Spain was in the setting up of specialist commercial theatres. This happened earlier in Spain and between 1565 and 1635, the year Lope de Vega died, a network of such theatres or "corrales" was established across nearly all Spanish cities and towns. They represented a happy combination of municipal planning and private enterprise. Municipalities granted the right to build and administer theatres to charities, and the charities in their turn acted as impresarios to the repertory companies, ploughing back the profits made from administering the theatres into their hospitals and almshouses. This gave the theatre in Spain a respectability which enabled it to shrug off attacks from the moralists of the day, a phenomenon as old as theatre itself. The Puritan Revolution closed down drama in England. In Spain all too many charities simply could not do without it.

Corrales were the yards enclosed by a block of houses, so this was not a street theatre but a yard theatre. The form dictated by building practise, was rectangular. A stage, with an apron projecting into the pit, would be built at one end of the rectangle. It tended to have its own roof, although the greater part of the spectators remained open to the sky, except for some roofing over seats at the side and the back, which were generally tiered. The windows of the houses giving on to the yard could, where appropriate, form boxes "aposentos" with rooms looking onto the stage, available for annual hire at a suitably extortionate price. The main bulk of the poorest spectators stood for the performance in the patio, where our word pit had its origin. At the back of the rectangle, the ground floor of the building giving on to the yard became converted into theatre entrances, separate ones for men and women, and a refreshment bar. The wealthy in the boxes did as they liked, but the rest of a Spanish audience was strictly segregated, seating for men only and seating for women only. As in Elizabethan theatres, one fee was charged for entrance and then an additional fee gave access to the more privileged parts of the audience accommodation. From 1574, right through into the eighteenth century, Madrid had two such theatres and the practise quickly spread throughout Spain. The stage was even more flexible than Shakespeare's. The projecting apron, the mid-stage, and the back stage, which could be curtained off were similar enough, but the back of the stage was a house with windows and balconies waiting to be used. For large scale battles, part of the pit could be roped off with ramps leading on to the stage, or an actor could jump from his real horse in the pit directly on to the stage before climbing up to a balcony at the back. "The furthest heaven of invention" could be the top balcony at the back of the stage, ready with its cloud machine for angels or the odd deus ex-machina to descend from the celestial sphere, while traps on the main stage could belch out the fumes of hell, spew up ghosts, or cover sudden disappearances in fire and thunder.

Performances were given in the afternoon, and if they ran late they risked a heavy fine. As in Elizabethan and Jacobean drama, a dance or mime to music opened the performance. In between the acts or "jornados" brief dance and mime plays were performed as in England, and the performance ended with more music and dance.

Once a performance started, there were no gaps to allow an audience to grow restive. Theatre audiences were uninhibited, and there was always an uneasy possibility of violence, probably not helped by the segregation of the sexes. It was exceptional for a play to run for more than a week. Two or three days was the norm, and with two theatres open all the year round in Madrid, only closing for Lent, the demand for new plays, if it did not create a new literary form, at least ensured that writers with talent arrived, as writers will, to make the most of the new opportunities and to jostle for a share of the funds newly available. Among them was a major talent, who was to extend and refashion the possibilities of the literary form and dominate the theatre during his lifetime. So much so that "es de Lope" entered the language as a common expression meaning "it's of real quality!" In El Greco's masterpiece, The Burial of the Conde de Orgaz, at Santo Tome, Toledo, where St Stephen and St Augustine have miraculously appeared at the funeral to lower the Count into his tomb, among the distinguished contemporaries watching the scene are three from the arts, Cervantes, Lope de Vega and El Greco himself. Philip II, although alive when it was painted is, of course, among the angels. Jan Morris wrote of this picture "it epitomises the alliance between God and the Spanish ruling classes . . . [who] expect miracles as a matter of policy and are watching the saints at work rather as they might watch any foreign expert sent to do a job." It is indicative of the importance of theatre, that Lope stands prominently amongst those very ruling classes. He may have been on the fringes of gentility by birth, but through his plays he could almost claim to rule the minds of whole generations of Spaniards.

As in England, theatres became associated with resident companies, only opening their doors to other touring groups when they themselves were summoned to perform at Court or for the local grandee. Touring companies, perceived as being of lesser quality than the resident companies, continued the rounds of great houses, inn yards and fairgrounds that had been the staple of touring companies throughout the Middle Ages. Resident companies, whose actors' lives were a source of wonder and gossip, maintained in their picaresque private lives that engaging mixture of sexual promiscuity and emotional insecurity which has tended to make backstage theatre life the human equivalent of a libidinous rabbit warren with weasels on the prowl. Each company was directed by a manager "autor de comedias", buying his plays from playwrights "poetas" or "ingenios". The company would have about eight actors and six actresses. Stars would be the "prima galan" and the "primera dama", and two clowns "graciosos" and two of the other men would expect to play older character parts.

As in England, drama was a poetic drama. Playwrights were "poetas". In the hands of Lope de Vega, however, the verse language heightened the drama in a complexity of structure more sophisticated than elsewhere. As he developed it during a richly productive life as a writer of plays from the early 1580's to 1630, his polymetric versification used separate metres and strophes for groups and categories of scenes, events or feelings. Unselfconsciously echoing ancient Greek drama, perhaps more by chance than by design, this produced much the same variety and complexity in dramatic language, contrapuntal effects in the verse akin to changes of tone in an orchestra, which it is quite impossible to reproduce in translation. Although the process began before Lope de Vega, and the polymetric system was refined even further after him, his work established a convention, adventurously explored its dramatic possibilities and accustomed audiences and other playwrights to the stimulating demands of such a complex literary form. He established other conventions too. The three act form became accepted in his time largely because he opted for it. He also developed the use of a sub-plot to complement the main plot, and built up the character of the "gracioso", the clown, who played an important part both in plot and sub-plot, and served both to bring comic relief, and to comment as an outsider on the action of the main plot so as to sharpen the audience's understanding and appreciation of the basic theme of the play.

He was amazingly productive. His protege Juan Perez de Montalban in his "Fama Postuma" claimed that Lope had written over 1800 plays for the "corrales" and over 400 "autos sacramentales", plays for religious festival performances. Even if these claims are far fetched, and modern scholarship contests them, careful academic researches by Morley and Bruerton and others tend to agree that we have 315 plays for the "corrales" that are unquestionably Lope's and of an additional 187 attributions, 27 are probably his, 87 probably not, while 73 are uncertain. Morley and Bruerton have done invaluable work in collating stylistic differences and developments, both to date the plays that are undoubtedly his and also to exclude for stylistic reasons plays incorrectly attributed. These, of course, are the plays that for one reason or another, have survived. Accepting a round number of something over 400 plays, this is in itself a staggering total. Imagine the daunting prospect for scholars if Shakespeare had written over 400 plays! Allowing a mere three weeks to study, analyse and make careful notes on each play, it would take a student six years of uninterrupted work simply to familiarise himself with the plays themselves. It is not surprising that academic experts on Lope de Vega are hardly elbowing for room on the campus.

Lope also wrote not only novels but, in his "Arte Nuevo de Hacer Comedias en Este Tiempo" published in 1609, a 389 line poem on the problems and skills involved in writing for the wide cross section of society that a typical "corrales" audience represented. It was not until the 1670's that English dramatic poets began to take criticism seriously and write treatises about writing plays as well as actually writing plays. Spain and France began earlier – Lope's poem shares much with Boileau's "Art Poetique" and both are indebted to Italy which began even earlier and was, in turn, dependent on the ancient Greeks. Lope is therefore very much a conscious part of the classical tradition. Indeed the first two decades of the seventeenth century endured a series of written attacks on Spanish drama for ignoring some of the classical rules and making up some of its own, and in a sense Lope's treatise is both a justification and an answer to classical purists. He was in the same difficult position that Dryden later found himself in. A large body of successful plays had established a dramatic form and a set of expectations in the audience which clearly broke some of the classical rules. To accept the classical rules was to condemn what common sense could not condemn. It was not until the later part of the seventeenth century that writers began to entertain the possibility that they might not only be as good as the ancients, but were possibly even better. Nobody had played with heretical notions like that since the Dark Ages engulfed Europe and the glory that was Greece and Rome, if shattered in fact, became all powerful as a mythology of past greatness. Lope sensibly sidestepped the question of the dramatic unities. While emphasising the unity of action, he completely ignored unity of place, and of time he recommended as short a time span as possible, except for history plays which by their nature spread themselves over years. Where possible he felt the action of each act should take place within the limit of a day. These are the confident tones of a seasoned practitioner in mid career, writing from experience of what works in the theatre as he knows it, aware of the classical tradition, feeling very much a part of it, but adapting and selecting, rather than slavishly obeying. It is like Wren's boldly inventive use of the classical architectural vocabulary for his own purposes, and very far from Burlington's stitching himself up in a straightjacket of classical rules.

Then there is the question of tragi-comedy. Plays for the "corrales" were known as "comedias". Literary historians until recently found it difficult to fit Spanish dramatists into the category called "tragedy", and so tended to find them unable to write it. Readers of the two plays in this book will know otherwise. Lope could write a powerful, serious tragedy as effectively as any other outstanding master of the theatre, but, like Shakespeare, he also introduced humorous scenes and events into a serious play, whenever it seemed appropriate, and he argued persuasively in favour of doing so, whatever the classical rules laid down. He was aware of the fierce controversy in Italy over Guarini's "Il Pastor Fido" written in the early 1580's, mixing tragedy and comedy and then vigorously defended by Guarini. Lope not only used some of Guarini's arguments, but the very success in Spain of "Il Pastor Fido" may well have influenced Lope's practice, particularly in the development of the "gracioso" and comic sub-plot to comment on the serious main narrative. The poem is full of shrewd, practical observations and advice for would-be playwrights. They should forget classical rules about not putting monarchs into comedies. After all Plautus had written a comedy "Amphitryon" and thought nothing of including Jupiter himself as a character. It was what was appropriate to the subject matter, once chosen, that mattered.

And who was this confident spokesman for Spanish drama, still with twenty six years of prolific writing ahead of him? First and foremost he was a poet, a spinner of magical words, but during his long writing career, from the early 1580's to 1635, he taught himself by trial and error the craft of writing plays. In his early days he clearly wrote with a fatal facility, and must have thrown off a play from a brimming creative imagination, seemingly without much thought and effort. Some of his early plays can seem almost naive in their inability to organise the talent always on display. But he learned quickly. What impresses always is the sheer power of his writing, a passionate appetite for life, a revelling in exuberance, in the joy and fun of living. He has tended to be categorised as the sensualist with a zest for life where his successor Calderon is seen as a thinker who relished the play of the intellect. This, however flattering to Calderon, is monstrously unfair to Lope, who was one of the most impressive and creative minds of his generation, who seems to have led as full and active a life in reality as in the imaginative world he created for the stage, who after more than his fair share of the fleshpots of physical pleasure became a priest, spanning in his own lifetsyles the contradictions inherent in the Renaissance between the older, if newly discovered, classical freedoms of the senses and the Christian emphasis on the mind and the soul.

The range of his plays in subject matter and style is sufficient tribute in itself to his zest for life, the breadth of his understanding, and his all encompassing imagination. While obviously the aim of seventeenth century Spanish drama was to entertain and give pleasure, there was also an evident belief that the drama taught its audiences lessons about life, gave them a better understanding of themselves, of the world around them, and of their relations with others. Since this was the "raison d'etre" of the religious drama the "autos sacramentales" co-existing with the popular theatre of the "corrales", and since the whole purpose of medieval art had been to instruct, this attitude was not surprising. Both audience and playwright expected a moral to be drawn. This made characterisation and action in seventeenth century drama subordinate to the main theme of the play.

The careful touches with which Shakespeare creates believable characters in realistic situations, and the subsequent bias towards naturalism in English theatre, towards making theatre as lifelike as possible in the eighteenth and nineteenth centuries were alien to what Spanish seventeenth century drama was attempting to do. A Spanish audience expected to see a theme running through a play, and indeed to see the play as the working out of that theme, so that it is the theme, rather than the action, which brings cohesion and unity to the play. What happens in the play is designed to emphasise the force of the main theme, and should be understood in those terms. This makes Spanish drama essentially a theatre of ideas, where what actually happens in the play, and the characters around whom the play appears to be constructed, are all designed to illustrate a set of ideas. Audiences came away from a Spanish play tending to think not along the lines of "if only Hamlet had been able to make up his mind" but pondering a general lesson, such as "how foolishly snobbery makes us behave". This is so even in Lope de Vega's most light-hearted and frothy plays, amorous intrigues with a lineage stretching back to Plautus and Terence. It certainly applies to the two of his most serious and best known plays included here. They are both tragedies and it may be useful to emphasise that Renaissance playwrights, particularly in Spain, tended to regard historical or biblical plays as serious plays. Events that had actually happened fitted more appropriately into the mould of tragedy, whereas an invented plot allowed free play for fantasy and imagination and was therefore more appropriate as comedy. However odd these assumptions may seem nowadays, they were an accepted seventeenth century convention in Spain. Dramatists certainly approached history with this apparent seriousness and respect, but it did not prevent them from altering the facts and reshaping the characters to make the theme more effective.

Both Lope's plays in this volume are taken from life and concerned with the difficult subject of honour, where attitudes taken for granted in the seventeenth century require more explanation in the twentieth. It hardly needs emphasising that there are two very different, almost mutually contradictory strands in our culture, which have persisted to the present. In my own schooling the two extremes of this cultural contradiction were made very clear. I attended a Christian boarding school with a school chaplain who took his duties very seriously and, looking back, I seem to have spent an inordinate time in a variety of religious services whose main aim seems to have been to set me down as part of an imprisoned congregation, while the chaplain thundered at us that this life was a vale of tears, a preparation for the life to come, and that if we were to win salvation in the after life, we must make strenuous efforts at all times to resist the Devil's blandishments in this one. If we had any pretensions to learning we were put, as previous generations of pupils had been for centuries, to study Latin and Greek. After we had reached a certain level of proficiency, we were exposed at the callow and impressionable age of fifteen and sixteen to classical authors in the original. These authors had a very different message for us. Life might be short, but while it lasted it could be unbearably sweet. Physical passion, the pleasure of the senses, the company of women, feasting and wine, music and conversation and, above all, the fascinating interplay of human relationships in love and friendship, these were what life had to offer. Intoxicated by such heady promises during the day in the classroom, we were then herded back into the stalls in chapel to be told all over again to resist temptation, put the Devil behind us, and concentrate firmly on confessing our sins of thought and deed, [alas largely in thought alone for most of us] to prepare for salvation in the after life. The system, particularly for the intelligent, the imaginative, and the sensitive, was schizophrenic beyond belief. And yet it faithfully represented what had been Christian culture since the Renaissance.

When the doctrines of Christianity conquered the minds and hearts of the classical world, most cultural historians would agree that the major shift in European sensibility which resulted was a change for the better. If we assume for the sake of argument that you, gentle reader, are a monster of sexual perversion, just for the sake of argument you understand, had you lived in classical Greece or Rome you could have wandered down into the market place, and provided you could produce the necessary cash, bought some attractive youngster of either sex on whom to practise your hideous perversions, and nobody would have dreamed of denying you such a right. The classical world was a slave society, a brutal and callous world, where a whole class of fellow human beings had almost no rights at all. Christianity with its concepts of equality before the Lord, of an individual soul to be respected, of mercy and forgiveness, of love and charity, civilised whole areas of human intercourse.

Unfortunately the whole civilisation which Christianity arrived to civilise was destroyed in waves of barbaric invasions. Europe disappeared, as far as history is concerned, into the Dark Ages, into general chaos, and the primitive society which emerged from the collapse, knew little or nothing of the grandeur or achievements of Greece or Rome, apart from the broken monuments still littering the landscape around them. Christianity survived and gradually converted the barbarians all over again. Medieval society was very much a third world society, primitive, technologically backward, superstitious, with an all powerful church which not only imposed a powerful ideological grip on the minds of everyone, but siphoned off what little surplus wealth there was for its own aggrandisement.

We tend to think of our culture as representing first the achievements of the Greeks and Romans, and then the triumph of the shift towards civilising values which Christianity brought. Actually it was not like that at all. Upon a primitive backward, superstitious, closed world "steeped in error", upon that medieval society, growing acquaintaince with Greek and Roman texts opened up the kind of fissures still apparent in my schooling. The Renaissance was exactly what the French word means, a rebirth of interest and enlightenment in things classical. Yet in many ways, classical ideas were diametrically opposed to medieval Christianity. Both had to try and adapt, and certainly by the seventeenth century, and some would maintain even by the twentieth century, there were still areas where one set of assumptions opposed another.

The concept of honour is one such battle ground. The classical Greeks had a highly developed sense of male personal honour. Schoolboys in Athens followed a curriculum that seems wonderfully simple in a later technological era. They learned to read and write, they did a little maths, some music, but otherwise their academic, as opposed to athletic studies, were restricted entirely to a study of Homer. The Greeks felt that Homer was in himself a complete education for life. This Bronze Age poet was in our terms, a powerful medium for communicating his society's dominant ideology. If we look at Homer's assumptions about honour, we are looking at a value system that was shared across all the Greek city states, a common set of attitudes and beliefs which bound them together, and kept them haughtily conscious of their superiority to the barbarians who made up the rest of the world.

On the Trojan expedition, about which Homer wrote in the Iliad, Achilles, the Greek hero, the personification of the concept of honour, saw himself as insulted by Agamemnon, the overall commander. The Greeks had captured cities and acquired booty en route to Troy, and in the share out of the plunder, a pretty slave girl Briseis, had originally been allocated to Achilles. Agamemnon decided to re-allocate the spoils, and in the redivision, he awarded Briseis to himself. Achilles therefore decided to sulk. When they arrived at Troy, Achilles and his troops took no part in the battles because Achilles felt himself to have been wronged, his honour insulted.

We, embedded in a twentieth century viewpoint, might think that he was "not pulling his weight", "not being a good member of the team", "thinking of himself before others", "selfishly putting himself first", but that was not how Homer and his audience saw it. A Greek hero jealously guarded his "reputation", what others thought of him, and his honour depended on that public respect. Slighted by Agamemnon, Achilles was suffering what a very similar Japanese code would call "a loss of face", and his first duty, in caring for his public reputation, was to make it clear that he would not countenance such an insult. [Notice the similarity in our own language between the Japanese "loss of face", and our refusal to "countenance" an injury.] The Greeks saw the heroic individual as being, first and foremost, careful to guard his public reputation, "jealous of his own honour", his status in his own society seen as dependent on his readiness to defend and, if necessary, fight for the respect of others.

Of course the hero had other attributes. In the Iliad the reader comes to admire the Trojan hero, Hector, and at the end of the Iliad the two heroes fight each other in individual combat. Indeed, most of the Greek-Trojan conflict is described by Homer in terms of individual combat. Finally, Hector, after a noble fight, is vanquished and lies defenceless on the ground, while above him Achilles stands, spear poised. Hector, understandably in the circumstances, pleads to be spared. We might think that Achilles should show generosity, magnanimity for such a brave and doughty opponent. Nothing of the sort. Achilles says the Homeric Greek equivalent of "no way" and in goes the spear, and Homer tells us in loving detail what it does on the way in, and what parts of Hector's anatomy are dragged with it on the way out. So much for Hector. Concepts of generosity, magnaminity, forgiveness, would be considered as weaknesses in classical Greek times. A hero is ruthless, competitive, prepared to step on others in order to get what he wants, judged by success "it's the results that count", and judged also by his readiness to jump to the defence of his public reputation, his status in the eyes of others, his own honour.

Christianity saw the hero in quite different terms. The Christian was, above all, attempting to imitate Christ. Concepts of forgiveness, generosity, charity, love of one's neighbour, turning the other cheek, were all at variance with what classical Greeks admired. The Christian was concerned with following Christ's teachings and attempting to do what was right in their terms. He wrestled with his own conscience, "a man has to do what a man has to do", irrespective of what others thought of him. He had to justify his behaviour to God, and to his own conscience, and the rest of society, his public reputation, came a very poor third in such a judgement. "Conscience doth make cowards of us all" is not a statement an ancient Greek could feel at home with.

The Christian view dominated Europe throughout the Middle Ages. It was built on the conversion of barbaric hordes who had their own concept of honour. The English jury system emerged from a whole set of Saxon concepts about an individual being worth the number of other men around him prepared to stand by him, concepts closer to classical Greece than to Christianity. But Christianity triumphed, and as the Dark Ages receded, and Europe prospered, the Middle Ages represented a triumph of Christian ideology. Charging interest on a loan was seen, throughout the Middle Ages, as being un-Christian and a crime. Only non-Christians like the Jews were allowed to get away with it. Charging more for something in a shop than it was worth was seen as un-Christian and a crime. Trying to pay a workman less than a fair wage was seen as un-Christan and a crime. However backward, primitive and superstitious medieval society was, some of its commonly held values seem remarkably attractive to us in retrospect. Economic historians would remind us, however, that throughout the Middle Ages, another battle was going on. The lay ruler, the monarch, the prince, the duke, was struggling for supremacy of power with the Church. By and large, the Church won this struggle for most of the Middle Ages. Spectacularly when, for example, Henry II was scourged by the monks at the shrine of Thomas a Beckett after walking barefoot in penance in 1174.

By the Renaissance, the Church was losing, partly because of its own corruption and venality. "All power corrupts" and the Church in the later Middle Ages became a vivid example of just how far power's corrupting influence can go. At the same time alien ideas had been spreading through Europe since as far back as 1085 when the fall of Toledo unleashed libraries of

Greek texts, carefully preserved in Arabic by Arab civilisation. Arab culture in Spain reached a high point, superior to backward Christian Europe in technology [there was public lighting in the streets of Cordoba], in toleration, different races and creeds lived freely together, and in scholarship, a careful preservation and adaptation of Greek writings, science and medicine. It was not until 1492, about the same time as the discovery of America, that the last Arab state in Spain was defeated and Arab influence no longer officially ruled anywhere in Spain. After the fall of Toledo the influence of Arab culture and the Greek culture it had made its own permeated European universities and centres of thought, such as the courts of enlightened monarchs, and gradually built into that ferment of new ideas values and assumptions we call the Renaissance. In the nineteenth century history was rewritten to imply that only when Constantinople fell to the Turks did fleeing scholars bring the precious texts of our European Greek and Roman heritage back to us. This conveniently eliminated the Arabs, who were not Europeans at all, and therefore seen as not being entitled to membership of the club. Indeed it did more, managing to indict the Turks for destroying Constantinople, one of the great cities of European civilisation. Actually Constantinople was sacked and its influence effectively destroyed by a Venetian-led European army, ostensibly on a Christian crusade, but actually out for whatever booty it could get in 1204. This sort of awkward fact never appeared in Victorian school history books.

Along with all the other bewildering rich echoes and assumptions from a forgotten classical world, Greek ideas about honour arrived at a remarkably convenient time to underpin the struggle for supremacy between Church and State in late medieval Europe. If the ruler and the state were to wrest control of economic power from the Church, as Henry VIII did in the dissolution of the monasteries, for example, they needed an alternative ideology, a set of values and assumptions which, while grudgingly allowing the Church to maintain its control over the so called "spiritual" aspects of life, effectively divorced it from much of the everyday business on which the growing prosperity of Europe depended. Classical Greek concepts of honour, alongside a clutch of other concepts, effectively established the difference between the aristocrat, the gentleman, the new representative of the power of the state, as opposed to the priest, the old representative of the power of the Church. The more different the new representative values and assumptions were seen to be, the more readily could it become clear that the priest, the old representative, was irrelevant in whole areas of such a changing world.

In England the extremes of this position were clear for all to see. Sir Thomas More was beheaded for not being able to adjust to the new order, for attempting to maintain the Church's old hegemony in a world where the Church was not only losing power with its actual territorial estates being confiscated, but where its influence was being increasingly confined within so-called "spiritual" boundaries. It was no accident that the drama became secularised in Shakespeare's time. This was a small part of a much larger social and cultural revolution.

In Spain, as in the rest of Catholic Europe, the revolution was subtler, arrived more slowly, and was never quite as effective as in Protestant Europe, but it was a revolution nevertheless. Once again it was no accident that the drama of the "corrales" became secularised, but the fact that some of the profits from this commercial, secular theatre were siphoned off into religious charities emphasises how much gentler, how much more imperceptibly the changes were introduced in catholic Spain. In England the jagged results of abrasive change could be harder to bear. "Hark hark, the dogs do bark, the beggars are coming to town" refers to the gangs of uprooted labourers and former monks who terrorised defenceless villages in late Tudor times. Spain suffered much less from this kind of social upheaval, but the alternative ideology of the aristocrat and gentleman arrived just as inexorably in the Spanish Renaissance, as it did elsewhere in Europe.

From the early Renaissance, handbooks on being a gentleman spread the new concepts with all the authority that a host of classical references and quotations could give them. Since Italy was the spearhead of the Renaissance, setting the tone for later developments in Spain as much as in England and Northern Europe, these textbooks on how to be an aristocrat were largely Italian. It was no surprise that one of the earliest and most influential, Castiglione's "The Book of the Courtier", given over forty editions in the sixteenth century after its first printing in Venice in 1528, was banned by the Spanish Inquisition in 1576. As usual the Inquisition knew what it was doing. These books were to dominate an important area of European thought. Indeed they took root in Spain faster and more radically than anywhere else. Spain was entering upon its Golden Age. If England's great period of commercial prosperity and territorial aggrandisement centred around the eighteenth and nineteenth centuries, Spain's was the sixteenth and seventeenth. The discovery of America and the granting by the Pope of much of its wealth and territory as a monopoly to Spain, meant that Spain became the siphon through which the wealth of the New World reached Europe. It brought problems too. Syphilis, endemic in America, spread to Europe. Inflation arrived with the vast consignments of silver bullion, itself accelerating the erosion of the old order, and underpinning the establishment of a new, monied class.

The new ideology was ready and waiting to fit this new class as neatly as their newly ostentatious suits of bejewelled clothes. The classical ideas of a gentleman, carrying the responsibility for protecting his own honour, and that of his family were carefully elaborated. Honour, or the public respect due to the virtuous man, was seen in theory at least as being as important as life itself. Without it, a man was socially lost, consigned to a social grave if not an actual one. Lost honour could be won back, sometimes by legal means, but generally by the spilling of blood. In the last analysis a man not prepared to die to defend his honour was seen as being without honour. A slight to a man's honour, or that of his family, however small in itself therefore became immediately and grimly important. A slap on the face, a push in a crowd, a chance remark could all become – if seen as public loss of honour – grounds for mortal combat. Hence the rise of duelling, still remarkably slap happy and unscientific in the seventeenth century, but by the eighteenth a nastily specialised set of skills which no would-be gentleman could do without. The code of honour became even more ritualised. Calling a man a liar was seen as being no more and no less grave than invading the sanctity of his own body space by pulling his beard. Neither of these were really any more or less a cause for demanding satisfaction than the seduction of a wife. Don Juan in another context, remarked cheerfully that, given the choice between pulling a man's beard and seducing his wife to give him grounds for a challenge, after careful and prolonged reflection, he was inclined to pursue the latter course. Certainly in Spain it was legal to avenge dishonour to oneself or one's family. Courts accepted the killing of both the seduced wife and the seducer, even where adultery was only suspected, provided such suspicions were public knowledge. The emphasis was always on a public reputation. As the Duke says in "Lost in a Mirror":

> But how can I find out
> What has gone on
> Without witnesses knowing
> My honour has gone?

The code of honour excluded not only the church, but Christian teaching. Where his honour was concerned, a gentleman brushed the Church aside. The priest's role was to bring the comforts of the last rites to the dying victim after satisfaction had been exacted. No set of rituals could more cleverly or more effectively have established the divisions between Church and State or reasserted more convincingly the values of classical Greece and Rome. These assumptions about the need to protect individual honour have persisted with amazing resilience. Even in the last century English politicians called each other out to fight private duels, as did Americans. The insistence in so many Hollywood films on the need for the hero to "prove himself", to establish his personal reputation and honour as a member of the group, makes it clear that, however garbled, Renaissance teachings about the role of the gentleman bit deep. It might surprise Clint Eastwood fans to know that his spaghetti westerns were faithfully reproducing fifteenth century Italian ideas of what a virtuous man should do protect his own standing in the eyes of those around him.

Both the plays in this volume are concerned with the concept of honour, and Lope de Vega wrote a number of other plays attempting to come to terms with what, in his own time, was a remarkably powerful and radical concept, at odds with many of the assumptions inherent in earlier Christian doctrine. In "Fuente Ovejuna" he tackles the subject head on. One of the most important aspects of the code of honour is that it is class-related. By accepting the obligations of the code, an aristocrat and a gentleman, just as much as an ancient Greek hero is distinguishing himself from the common herd. What is all right for ordinary people is not all right for him. He has to be jealous of his honour, ready at any time to put his very life at hazard in its defence. We can remember that Aristotle felt it was this willingness to hazard the most precious commodity we possess, life itself, which made being a soldier a more honourable profession than any other. By participating in and belonging to the gentlemanly code from the Renaissance onwards a gentleman cloaked himself in the same mystique that surrounded the medieval knight of chivalry, or Aristotle's soldier. In "Fuente Ovejuna" Lope de Vega asked the unanswerable question; why is the peasant villager not allowed his share of honour, his share of reputation, his share of public respect? Fernand Gomez sneers "your honour" at the peasants who seem to be getting ideas above their station and this is the voice of aristocratic privilege taunting those beyond the pale. Lope is asking his audience to think about the true nature of honour. That is the main theme of "Fuente Ovejuna". It has other themes too which we shall look at, but in asking his audience to reflect on honour, Lope is echoing the advanced thought of his day. Gomez, the Comendador, is a despicable tyrant, and the villagers agree not only to his killing but, by their mutual collective silence afterwards, they prevent the authorities from discovering his murderer. The audience is in no doubt that Gomez deserved to die. They admire the villagers' determination to stand together after it. These are honourable men, committed to an honourable course of action.

Lope is edging his audience towards thinking that true honour depends not on class, not on noble birth, but on virtuous action. The accident of birth at best implies an obligation to behave virtuously, but virtue is won by actions and the man or woman deserving honour is the one whose deeds have earned respect, irrespective of social class. It is not the result or the success that matters, so much as the intention, the determination and fortitude shown in attempting to realise them. This is a sophisticated view of honour. It still accepts many classical assumptions which are basically pre-Christian. It is right to kill the Comendador, and honour consists in not only killing him but in standing by each other afterwards. In accepting this, the audience still see the shedding of blood as conferring honour. But at least Lope is attacking the idea of class, the idea that honour is an aristocratic preserve. The play's assumptions are that every man or woman, whatever their status in society, can win honour and reputation and self respect. Indeed, it is a woman, rather than a man, who finally shames the villagers into action, shame being bound up with honour, the woman personifying the reputation they will have to live with, as her husband will have to live with her, for the rest of their lives. Virtue in the play is shared equally between the king and the villagers. The wrongdoer is the Comendador. Virtue and vice, honour and dishonour are seen to have little or nothing to do with barriers of class, birth and social position. In the claustrophobic and semi-feudal snobberies of the seventeenth century Spanish class system, the play must have seemed radical indeed.

The peasants are, of course, idealised. The grim actualities of their hard lives do not form part of the dramatists intentions. They belong to the bucolic pastoral, a strand in European literature tracing its wayward path back to Horace's "Beatus Ille", which has persistently refused to be anything but sentimental about shepherds and agricultural workers. There are recognisable echoes and allusions in Lope's poetry making these antecedents clear, and even more irritatingly reaching some of the high points of his verse. But it is no good interposing a twentieth century desire for realism for facing the hard facts of how tough actual village life must have been. In seventeenth century drama characters and actions are subordinated to the theme. This is a theatre of ideas and of poetry, and if real life does not fit, it is left outside like the muddy boots the farmer discards at the door.

There are other ideas in "Fuente Ovejuna". The discussion in Act I between Barrildo and Mengo about love crystalises the secondary theme which underpins the play's main analysis of honour. As the villagers stand by each other, they learn, as does the audience, the importance of being able to trust each other, that love and confidence which the play reassuringly asserts as a vital bond to link disparate elements of society together. Here Lope and his audience are harking back to an earlier Christian medieval view of society, welded together in love and trust from the highest to the lowest, each doing his best in the station fate has allotted. "The rich man in his castle, the poor man at his gate". In the twentieth century, it seems even more idealised than the bucolic pastoral element, a charmingly naive view of a society that will never change, where the king rules through divine right, where the nobility by the accident of birth have higher responsibilities thrust upon them, which it is their duty to live up to, and where the cheerful yokel, doffing his cap to his betters, earns wide respect through hard work and pleasing humility. It seems incredible in the seventeenth century, when social change was proceeding at a faster rate than for hundreds of years previously, audiences went for this self-deluding nonsense. Yet they undoubtedly did. Just as the Church reassured them about the fundamental righteousness of their society, so this medieval view of the

nature of the state, suitably backed by church teaching, helped to shield them
from the realities of social change until long after the changes had actually taken
place. In learning collective trust and love, putting their community before
their own self-interest, the villagers are learning in the play about the love of
God, whose representatives the king and queen are, and whose pardon has as
much force in changing the outcome of the play, as the priestly pardon brings
to the individual in the confessional. It brings the play to its second high point.
We know from his "Arte Nuevo" that Lope accepted the classical view of the
development of the plot from protasis [exposition] to epitasis [complication]
and catastrophe [unravelling], and his three act form generally fits this mould
neatly enough. But in "Fuente Ovejuna" the thrilling high point of the
Comendador's death is followed by the cerebral high point of the play's
resolution, and whatever we may think of the values which underpin it, it
rounds off the drama with an exhilarating and satisfying sense of completeness.
The theme has worked itself out in a logical and coherent way, appealing in its
development to both the hearts and the minds of the audience.

The poetic metaphors of the play use a range of animal imagery which
probably had an immediacy in the seventeenth century which an urban
industrialised twentieth century has lost. Gomez names Frondoso dog, and as a
metaphor for faithfulness that is acceptable enough, but it is Gomez who is seen
as a running dog, to be killed like a dog. Simile and metaphor are the stock in
trade of a poet, but Lope builds his dramatic effects with a verbal language
whose subtlety adds layers of richly textured meanings and ironies. Add to
these the skilful varieties and carefully chosen range of his polymetric system to
emphasise and isolate out different aspects of situation and emotion and we can
only admire the level of sophistication in a tragic drama which can grapple with
such intellectually demanding subject matter and find the theatrical meanings
and the language to measure up to the challenge of its theme.

"Lost in a Mirror" is a late play written in 1631. It took its plot from a novella
by Bandello which was itself based on a real life incident. It made, therefore, a
fit subject for tragedy, its authenticity giving it a gravitas for seventeenth
century Spain which mere fantasy, created by an author's imagination, could
never acquire. Whatever we may think of this artificial distinction, it
predisposed audiences to take the subject matter seriously if they knew the
events echoed historical reality, just as modern cinema audiences are
sometimes assured at the beginning of a film that the events depicted are a "true
story". Even today Hollywood could hardly introduce a comedy in this way, and
it is this distinction which Spanish audiences and playwrights clearly felt was
crucial.

There are three central characters and Lope makes no attempt to idealise any
of them. They are presented as fully rounded, believable individuals, each

striving to lead a satisfactory life, but each flawed by weakness which ultimately destroys. The Duke of Ferrara's weakness is plain for all to see. He has a bastard son, and his cheerful womanising is spelled out early in the play. Once again the metaphors are those of the countryside:

> The Duke looks,
> Just like a fox.

And when he can appear in public as somebody else, then the sensualist can forget his public reputation and honour:

> When you're in disguise,
> Nothing's forbidden, anything goes.

So the Duke can:

> Dance to love's tune
> On the tiles of the Moon

The fact that the Duke is married does not prevent his happy whoring. Nor is there any suggestion in this play that his wife's honour is besmirched by his infidelity, that she requires satisfaction, that only the death of husband and mistress can satisfy the wrong done to her. The double standard, which had existed throughout the Middle Ages, was still largely unquestioned in the seventeenth century. What was acceptable behaviour in a man, was certainly not acceptable, was indeed unheard of, in a woman. A man's honour was bound up in his wife's chastity, but the reverse was not even feasible. Nothing could more clearly indicate the subordinate status of women in European society, a general view of them as male chattel than their humble role in the relative hierarchies of the codes of honour. While the Duke is away on a Papal war, something perceived as an honourable Christian activity, his bastard son begins an affair with the Duke's wife. According to the codes of the time, this was incest. Their act of love represents the weakness of the other two central characters, the bastard and the Duchess. The son is betraying his father's trust, as is the wife. Enmeshed in the code of honour, as was the rest of Spanish society, the Duke's first aim on discovering the wrong done him when he returns from the war, is to keep the matter secret:

> This is what the laws of honour
> say! That there must never be
> public knowledge of my injury
> for that would double my dishonour.

One of the many ironies in the situation is that the Duke is betrayed, not by a legal son, but by his own bastard, by the very evidence of the Duke's own fall from grace. In that fall he created the instrument to punish himself for doing so. It is a neat twist that a Catholic, Spanish audience would relish to the full. "The evil that men do lives after them" with a vengeance. The Duke has returned from the war a changed man, ready to live honourably and cherish his wife. The blow, when he discovers how she has cheated him, is akin to the discovery of AIDS in the twentieth century. The knowledge leads inexorably to death. It is not a question of whether, but where and how and when. Acting in his capacity as a ruler and judge, he decrees a punishment that he and his audience see as inevitable and just. The son is persuaded to kill the wife in error, and then himself punished for the murder. The Duke's public reputation remains untouched and he has managed to preserve his own private sense of honour as well. The Duke's punishment is clear enough. He has killed his own son. He has lost the virtuous wife he thought he possessed. That the public sense of his honour and reputation remained intact, must have seemed a hollow sham even for seventeenth century Spain:

> Honour my fierce enemy!
> Who invented your cruel maze?

Lope was here asking questions that were unanswerable in seventeenth century terms. Just as in Greek tragedy we watch the hubris of the proud man slowly ground to dust by the force of circumstances over which he has no control, squirm and struggle as he may, so the options open to the Duke leave him equally little choice. He is left at the end of the play facing a bleak future, and yet his audience might well have pondered as they left the theatre, how could it have been otherwise? The code of honour required him to act as he did. Had he been a virtuous man, there would have been no bastard in the first place, so he lives betrayed by his own weakness. The moral is clear. That the son should have betrayed his father so monstrously is spelled out as weakness. The son's willingness to desert the Duchess for another marriage on his father's return shows him in the same mould as his father, ready to use women, surrendering to the pleasures of an affair, and then move on. The audience could share his pleasure in the affair and find his actions all too believable, but ultimately they had to condemn him as shallow in his love which could not weigh in the balance against the betrayal of his father. He was seen to deserve his fate. For us Casandra, the wife, is perhaps the most sympathetic of the three protagonists:

> Because of the wrongs done by the Duke
> My soul leans towards wickedness.
> I'm like a mad woman trying to take
> Revenge and pleasure at the same time.

She here justifies her behaviour because of the wrongs done to her by her husband, and for a modern audience this seems justification enough. It has to be stressed that this would have seemed mere sophistry for Lope's Spanish audience. It could never have aroused the sympathy it undoubtedly arouses today. Fidelity and purity were so bound up in being a wife and mother, that her fall would have been complete in Spanish eyes. A Spanish audience, watching her become a wicked woman, would consider her fate as deserved as it was inevitable.

It is Lope's skill as a playwright that this ancient package of outmoded conventions and assumptions still works in the theatre. The issues are presented so straightforwardly and the characters, even they if exist for us only in a strange time warp, are so believable they persuade us to share, for the brief excitement of the drama, their alien view of the world and its twisted obligations. It is a strange reversal of time that just as Lope could respond to the force of classical drama from an entirely different standpoint – that of a seventeenth century Spaniard with pretensions to gentility – so we in the twentieth century can respond to the force of Lope and to the influence of classical drama upon him, while sharing even less of his views than he had in common with the pagan world.

For Lope's audience "Lost in a Mirror" was most decidedly not a tragedy about a doomed couple. The tragedy was the Duke's, and the tangled web through which the weakness of each of the three main characters helped to destroy the other two. As in most seventeenth century drama, character and action served to illustrate the theme and it remains a theatre of ideas, challenging us to puzzle out the ideas inherent in the drama, inviting us to ponder the moral in the play, which remains paramount. Once an honourable man stoops to dishonour, he may retain a mask of public reputation, but his life becomes a hollow sham, and he is really no better than anybody else who surrenders to temptation. It is a bleak message. Although Lope ended his life as a priest, there is no hint in this play of redemption or forgiveness. The code of honour co-existed alongside church teaching, and made few connections with it. In a period still dominated by the church, the theatre of the "corrales" was ostensibly "real life". Yet with the hindsight the twentieth century brings, we can see that Lope and his audience had a warped view of "real life", a world where a man's honour justified his killing wife and lover, and where legal courts accepted such actions as just and worthy, while in the next street, churchgoers sat raptly listening to sermons about turning the other cheek, loving one's enemies, and forgiving them, while making mental reservations that, of course, this did not apply where a man's honour was concerned, might seem at first glance rather far removed from our own. Yet the incompatibility between the pagan and the Christian world still persists, if weakened, in our own time. Its echoes are all around us. They are still strong enough for us to sympathise with Lope's characters, even while we tell ourselves that, of course, things are altogether different now. It is like responding to tunes and songs from armies in half forgotten wars. The music still works, even though we have forgotten, or never knew, the words. Lope is above all a poet and his siren voices still enchant.

NICHOLAS DROMGOOLE

Fuente Ovejuna

This version of *Fuente Ovejuna* was commissioned by the National Theatre and first performed at its Cottesloe Theatre on 10 January 1989 with the following cast:

Commander Fernando Gomez de Guzman	James Laurenson
Captain Flores	Patrick Drury
Sergeant Ortuno	Jim Barclay
Grand Master Rodrigo Tellez Giron	Mark Lockyer
Laurencia	Rachel Joyce
Pascuala	Joy Richardson
Jacinta	Katharine Schlesinger
Frondoso	Wilbert Johnson
Mengo	Clive Rowe
Barrildo	Jonathan Cullen
Juan Rojo	Tam Dean Burn
Esteban	George Harris
Alonso	Alan Downer
Leonelo	Glyn Pritchard
Cimbranos	Nicholas Blane
Queen Isabella of Castile	Ellen Thomas
King Ferdinand of Aragon	Michael Jayes
Don Manrique	David Beames
First alderman	Simon Needs
Second alderman	Trevor Sellers
The farmer	David Michaels
Soldier	Trevor Sellers
A boy	Tim Mathews
Women	Sandra Butterworth, Laura Shavin

Director   Declan Donnellan
Designer   Nick Ormerod
Lighting   Mick Hughes
Sound   David E. Smith
Production Manager   Jason Barnes
Stage Manager   Sarah Parkin
Deputy Stage Manager   Alison Rankin
Assistant Stage Managers   Jane Suffling, Peter MacCoy
Costume Supervisor   Angie Burns
Publicist   Stephen Wood

Act 1

Scene 1

[*An ante-chamber in the house of the* MASTER *of the Order of Calatrava – a powerful organisation which takes as its insignia a red cross*]

[*Enter* COMMANDER *Fernando Gomez de Guzman of the Order. He is dynamic, in his early forties, a successful and ruthless soldier*]

[*With him are his permanent aides – the young Captain* FLORES *and the veteran Sergeant* ORTUNO. *They have been travelling.* SOLDIERS *stand on guard*]

Commander	Does the Grand Master know I'm here?
Flores	He knows.
Ortuno	He's seventeen, sir. It's an arrogant age.
Commander	Does he know Fernando Gomez is waiting?
Flores	He doesn't know much. He's only a lad.
Commander	He's old enough to respect my rank.
Ortuno	He's one boy surrounded by a hundred advisers. They're telling him: Don't play favourites, take your time, Keep your distance and keep them waiting.
Commander	They ought to teach him a few old proverbs: "Punctuality is the politeness of kings".
Flores	Be rude to an equal – that's stupidity. Be rude to a lesser man – that's tyranny.
Commander	Lesser man? Am I less a man Than this pubescent?
Ortuno	He's new to all this, sir. He'll learn.
Commander	He'd better learn fast. Power brings obligations. When he was eight years old they presented him With the great sword of Calatrava And the Red Cross of our Order

                    Was pinned, in burning rubies, on his breast.
                    That day alone should have taught our Master
                    Something about courtesy.

Ortuno   If you feel insulted, we'd better leave.

Commander   I want to see what the boy's made of.

                    [*Enter the Grand* MASTER *of Calatrava and his following, which*
                    includes GUARDS *and* ADVISERS]

Master   Commander, I'm sorry, you must forgive me –
                    Fernando Gomez.

                    [MASTER *embraces* COMMANDER]

                    I've only just been told of your arrival.
                    For me to keep you waiting –
                    You must be furious.

Commander   Well, I'm used to respect, I value respect
                    And you, Grand Master, owe me some respect
                    For my loyalty and my battle-scars.

Master   I owe you more than I can ever repay.
                    I honour you and, once again, embrace you.
                    Brave Fernando.

                    [MASTER *embraces* COMMANDER *again*]

Commander   Well, I have risked my neck for you
                    And once, that time when the Pope was angry,
                    I intervened for you.

Master   It's true, I remember
                    And, by the holy crosses on both our breasts,
                    I honour you as I honour my father.

Commander   I'm pleased with you, Rodrigo.
                    Yes, you seem more mature –

Master   – But this is not a social visit . . .
                    I think your message said – military matters?

Commander   Listen to me. I'll explain
                    What your next move has to be.

Master   I'm listening, Commander.

Commander   Grand Master, you were raised
                    To your high office by the worth
                    Of your illustrious father.

He named you his successor
As the Grand Master of our Order.
As such it is your duty to support
King Alonso of Portugal
In his rightful claim to all Castile.

Master   King Ferdinand and Queen Isabella
Claim the same lands, of course.

Commander   But their claim's muddy. It's fraudulent.
Besides, you're related to King Alonso.
So I'll presume to offer some advice.
Assemble all the Knights of Calatrava.
Lay siege to the city of Cuidad Real
And capture it, then you'll control
The vital pass which is the gateway
From Andalusia into Castile.
You won't need many men.
You'll only be opposed
By shopkeepers, beggars
And a fistful of minor aristocrats
Pledged to Ferdinand and Isabella.

Don Rodrigo, they say you're just a boy.
They say the red cross is too heavy
For adolescent shoulders.
They are liars. Of course. But you have to prove it.
Remember your great ancestors –
The lords of Uruena and Villena.
Draw your great sword and let it slice
Into the red flesh of our enemies.
When that white sword is running with blood
The whole world will salute you.

Master   Fernando Gomez, rest assured –
I will support my kinsman.
Your summary, I think, is a little biased
And yet justice is on your side.

Since Cuidad Real must be captured
I'll take that city like a thunderbolt.

They say I am young.
Yes, I am young.
But my eyes are clear
And my heart is strong.
With the cross on my breast

Into battle I'll ride
And the white of my sword
Shall be reddened by blood.

Commander, do you have many soldiers?

Commander   Not many, but they're all hand-picked.
They can fight. I call them my lion-pack.
The men and women of Fuente Ovejuna
Are peasants. They're not trained at all –
Except in the use of sickles, forks and spades.

Master   Fuente Ovejuna? Is that your headquarters?

Commander   Just a shabby old town up in the hills.
My country house is there. It's my fortress too.

Master   Summon my soldiers.

Commander   Cuidad Real will collapse.

Master   That's right, Commander. Let's consult the maps.

Scene 2

[*The Town Square of Fuente Ovejuna. One public building with pillars. A couple of trees. Benches in the shade. Old houses. A spring which pours into a large drinking trough on wheels*]

[*Enter* LAURENCIA *and* PASCUALA, *two young peasant women, fetching water from the spring*]

Laurencia   I hope we've seen the last of that Commander.

Pascuala   Now there's a funny thing.
I had the feeling
That you were slightly put about
When he rode off.

Laurencia   Put about? I hope to God
We're rid of him for good.

Pascuala   Laurencia, I've seen plenty of women
As proud as you and harder to please,
But their little hearts betrayed them –
Slippery as candle-grease.

Laurencia   My heart's as dry as an old oak tree
And that's how it's going to stay.

Pascuala   Come on, it's daft even to think:
There is some water I'd never drink.

Laurencia	I swear by the sun that I never will,
	Though Fuente Ovejuna drinks its fill.
	Pascuala, what'd be the point
	In going to bed with Commander Gomez?
	Is he likely to marry me?
Pascuala	Not in this world.
Laurencia	How many of the local girls
	Have listened to the Commander's promises,
	Taken a walk in the woods and tottered back
	All tears and belly?
Pascuala	I've lost count.
	But it'll be a miracle
	If you escape that cunning bastard.
Laurencia	Don't bet on that!
	The Commander's chased me for more than a month
	And all he's got to show for it is blisters.
	His two friends, that Captain Flores
	And crafty old Sergeant Ortuno,
	Offered me a pair of yellow shoes
	And a silver necklace with doves in flight
	And a sort of spiderweb silky dress.
	They went on and on and on and on
	About their wonderful Commander,
	On and on till I was scared, Pascuala.
	But they can't do anything to break me down.
Pascuala	Where did this happen?
Laurencia	Down by the river where we wash the clothes.
	Down by the river six days ago.
Pascuala	Laurencia, I wouldn't die of horror
	If one day you surrendered.
Laurencia	You think I'm a spring chicken?
	No. I'm a tough little hen.
	And I'll chase Commander Gomez out of my backyard.
	He can crow somewhere else.
	[*Sings*]I'd rather
	Get up at daybreak
	And light up the fireplace
	Stack plenty of dry wood beside it.
	And then

Make a tortilla
The size of a cartwheel
With cupfuls of basil inside it.

I'd rather
Set the pot frothing
With rabbit and cabbage
United with garlic and spices.
And then
Fix up a marriage
Between some good bacon
And hundreds of aubergine slices.

I'd rather
Walk in the sunset
And pick me a necklace
Of grapes on the vine
Green and glowing.
And then
Heat up a pork chop
With olives and peppers
And anything else that is going.

I'd rather
Go to bed weary
With belly contented
And heart free of all obligation.
And then
Fall asleep praying
For more food the next day:
Deliver us, Lord, from temptation.

Pascuala –
You know these villains
They wheedle and woo us
And promise their love's to be trusted
And then
Call round at nightfall
Play with us till cockcrow
Then leave us and say they're disgusted.

Pascuala   You're right Laurencia.
When men cease to love you
They become unpleasant
As the ungrateful sparrow
To the generous peasant.

Laurencia	So sing me the story, Pascuala.
Pascuala	[*Sings*] In winter, when the fields are ice The sparrow longs to eat. He flies down from the roof and lands Beside the peasant's feet. He opens up his trembling beak And calls the peasant "sweet". Sweet! Sweet! He calls the peasant sweet.

That's how the sparrow earns his crumbs
Amid the snow and sleet,
But when the springtime swings around
And all the world's on heat,
The sparrow dances on the roof
And calls the peasant "Cheat".
Cheat! Cheat!
He calls the peasant cheat.

And men are sparrows when they long
To lay us on a sheet.
We are their life, their everything,
Their soul and their heartbeat.
But when they're cooler, they begin
To call the woman "cheat".
Cheat! Cheat!
And things I'll not repeat.

Laurencia	I remember a line from some ancient poem: Don't trust men farther than you can throw 'em.

[*Enter three young peasant men from the town* – FRONDOSO, *who is in love with Laurencia,* BARRILDO *and* MENGO, *who is somewhat stout.* MENGO *takes a bottle of wine which he has previously left to cool in the drinking trough, uncorks it, swigs and passes it round among his friends*]

Frondoso	Give up, Barrildo, he'll never give in.
Barrildo	Well, here's a pair of qualified judges. They're always ready to say what's right, Or, more likely, what's wrong.
Mengo	Before you ask them, let's make a deal. If they decide I'm right, You both have to give me some sort of prize For winning the debate.

Barrildo   Done. But, Mengo, suppose you lose.
                      What've you got to give to us?

Mengo   My little pipe. [*Produces penny whistle*]
                      It's worth more than a full granary –
                      It gives me more pleasure, anyway.

Barrildo   I'll shake on that.

                      [BARRILDO *and* MENGO *shake hands*]

Frondoso   Beautiful morning, lovely ladies!

Laurencia   Frondoso, are you calling us ladies?

Frondoso   It's just the modern manner of speech –
                      All students today are called "intellectuals".
                      Misers are "economical"
                      And the deaf are "hard of hearing".
                      If you're loudmouthed, they say you're "powerful",
                      The busybody "cares about people",
                      A bully is "strong-willed"
                      And a raving maniac is "so original".
                      So if you catch the pox, call it a "cold sore".
                      If you're a hunchback, call yourself "round-shouldered".
                      That's the fashion and I'm in the fashion
                      Up to my neck when I call the pair of you
                      "Ladies". Ladies, shall I go on.

Laurencia   I suppose, Frondoso, that in the city
                      People would frame that speech and hang it on their walls.
                      Well, I'm just a peasant and I wouldn't feed it to the pigs.

Frondoso   Explain to me where I'm wrong, learned Laurencia.

Laurencia   You're looking at it the wrong way up.
                      Let me tell you how people are judged.

                      A serious person is called "boring".
                      Those who seek justice are "heretics".
                      You keep your promise – you're "old-fashioned".
                      Be polite – "what an awful crawler!"
                      You give to a beggar – "hypocrite".
                      You're generous to everyone – "Ostentatious!"
                      If a woman tells the truth
                      She's called a bitch
                      But if she won't go to bed with you –
                      Call her a snobbish whore.
                      And a wife who's faithful – but that'll do.
                      Frondoso – have I silenced you?

Mengo	The devil's got into her tongue.
Barrildo	She's as tough as leather And cold as scandal.
Mengo	Send for a priest With a bell, book and candle.
Laurencia	What was your famous debate about?
Frondoso	I'll tell you, but can you listen?
Laurencia	There's no wax in my ears.
Frondoso	But seriously – we must settle a bet.
Laurencia	What's the wager?
Frondoso	Barrildo and I say Mengo's wrong.
Laurencia	And what does Mengo say?
Barrildo	Mengo denies the existence of something Which is obviously indispensable.
Mengo	No. I simply say that it doesn't exist Because I know it doesn't exist.
Laurencia	Please – somebody translate from Mengoese.
Barrildo	He says there's no such thing as love.
Laurencia	Most people find they can't manage without it.
Barrildo	Love is a madness, but I agree. Without love, the world would shut up shop.
Mengo	In the old days, they used to imagine That before the world came, there was Chaos. Now Chaos was made up of whizzing atoms And all the atoms were fighting each other. But one day Love crept in the back door And Love linked all the atoms together And that was the end of Chaos. Do you follow me?
Barrildo	And so everything in this world Harmonised with everything else. Which proves my point, for harmony Is only another word for love.
Mengo	One moment, Barrildo. Listen to this. First let me say I don't deny The existence and importance of <u>self-love</u>.

Self-love rules the universe,
Self-love maintains the balance of nature.
No, I've never denied, not for one minute
That we all have a kind of love we're born with
Which helps us to survive.
If you try to thump me on the nose
My hand flies up automatically,
My eyelashes slam their shutters
To protect my eyes
And my feet start sprinting away
To save my invaluable hooter.
But all this is <u>self-love</u>, not love itself.

Pascuala   Where does that leave the argument?

Laurencia   Up a fig tree.

Mengo   No, my point is, there's no greater love
Than that of man for his own self.

Pascuala   Sorry, Mengo, but you're wrong.
The passion with which a man loves a woman
Or a lion loves a lioness
Or a buck rabbit loves a doe –
That passion's real, you can't deny it.

Mengo   But that's not love at all.
That's what I call self-love.
Tell me, Laurencia, what is love?

Laurencia   To love is to desire

Mengo   Good. To love is to desire what?

Laurencia   To desire beauty.

Mengo   Beauty – yes – but why should love want beauty?

Laurencia   To enjoy it.

Mengo   Precisely.
And this enjoyment the lover hopes to have –
Is it not for himself?

Laurencia   It is.

Mengo   Therefore, because he loves himself
He pursues beauty, hoping to catch it,
So it will make him happy?

Laurencia   That is true.

Mengo	Since this is so, The love we're talking about Is the love I pursue For my own pleasure. It's all for me, myself. Self-love. You see?
Barrildo	The other day Father Oliver preached About another thinker like you called Plato. Now Plato had a great deal to say On the subject of love and what to do about it. Plato saved all of his love for the soul And the virtue of the person he loved.
Pascuala	Yes, there are colleges in the cities Overflowing with similar old men Who spend all day and half the night Discussing love. They're called philosophers And they get paid for it.
Laurencia	I will pronounce my verdict. Barrildo's right about Barrildo And Mengo's right about himself. Mengo, thank your lucky stars That you don't know what love is.
Mengo	Laurencia, do you love anybody?
Laurencia	Oh I love my virtue. I'm just like Plato.
Frondoso	May God punish you for that remark By striking you with jealousy.
Barrildo	Who won the debate?
Mengo	Who won the bet?
Pascuala	Take your problem to Father Oliver, I think he knows something about love. But if he can't oblige, write a nice letter To Don Plato at the university. Laurencia's never been in love And I've only a passing acquaintance with it – So how can we be judges?
Frondoso	By making fun of us poor men. Oh it's a wicked business when The sheet of paper mocks the pen.

[*Enter Captain* FLORES]

Flores   Beautiful morning, ladies and gentlemen.

Pascuala   Here comes the Commander's ploughboy.
                    Master comes later to sow the seed.

Laurencia   Sir, you're a polite sort of vulture today –
                    Where have you flown in from?

Flores   From the battle, sweetheart, isn't that obvious?

Laurencia   Will Commander Gomez be coming back?

Flores   He's well. The fighting's finished with now.
                    But it cost us plenty in blood and friends.

Frondoso   What happened, Captain?

Flores   I saw it. I was there.
                    Our mission was to capture Cuidad Real.
                    The Grand Master assembled his forces:
                    Two thousand vassals as soldiers on foot.
                    Three hundred Brothers of the Order
                    Riding on horseback, red crosses blazing.

                    Our brave young Master rode out that day
                    In a green cloak embroidered with gold
                    Fastened with silken cords over his bright armour.
                    A magnificent horse, well-fleshed and firm,
                    A dappled silver-grey like a gale-born cloud,
                    A steed raised on the clear water of the Betis river
                    And the deep rich grasses of its meadowbanks,
                    Its tail was covered by plaited strips
                    Of cunningly-worked leather, and its mane
                    Tied in tight curls with whitest ribbons
                    Which matched the snow-flake marks
                    Flecking his pale grey flanks.

                    At his right hand rode Commander Gomez,
                    Your overlord, upon a sturdy
                    Stallion the colour of crystallised honey,
                    With a jet-black mane and tail, but a white underlip.
                    The Commander wore a cloak
                    Of flowing, orange-coloured silk
                    With golden tracery and milky pearls.
                    His white-plumed helmet seemed to be
                    Bursting with orange blossom, and he bore
                    That famous pine-tree of a lance
                    Before which proud Granada trembles.

                    We advanced, through the dust, towards Cuidad Real.

The city fathers were stubborn.
They took up arms
Shouting "For Ferdinand and Isabella!/"
They fought hard, but we beat them down.
Our young Master gave his orders.
Rebel leaders were beheaded.
Their followers were gagged and flogged through the streets.
Now the city fears him, the city admires him,
For a youth so suddenly turned conqueror
Will surely grow into a giant
Who will become the scourge of Africa
And overcome a million crescent moons
With his triumphant cross of blood.

He has been generous, too,
Heaping rare gifts upon us,
And he let us plunder the city as freely
As if it were his private property.

But here comes our Commander. Greet him joyfully.
Your smiles and cheers must crown his victory.

[*Enter the* COMMANDER *with Sergeant* ORTUNO, SOLDIERS, MUSICIANS,
local councillors including JUAN ROJO, *and the joint Mayors
of Fuente Ovejuna,* ALONSO *and* ESTEBAN. *Esteban is also Chief
Magistrate and is the father of Laurencia*]

People of Fuente Ovejuna
[*Sing*]
Welcome the Commander
Who killed our enemies
Welcome the Commander
For he beat them to their knees

Long live Commander Gomez
Who is terrible in war
But in peacetime he is peaceful
May he live for evermore

Long live Commander Gomez
Our mighty overlord
For he cut up the rebels
With his celebrated sword

Now he comes back to Fuente
For this is where his home is
We hope he stays for ever
Long live Commander Gomez!

Commander   People of Fuente Ovejuna
                  I thank you with all my heart
                  For the affection you have shown today.

Alonso   Commander, our town has only shown
                  A little part of its true feelings.

Juan Rojo   Commander, Senor Esteban,
                  Who is our Chief Magistrate
                  And joint Mayor with Alonso here
                  Would like to make a presentation.

Commander   I am obliged to him. Proceed.

Mengo   [*To* ESTEBAN]
                  Here's the speech I wrote for you.

                  [ESTEBAN *clears his throat and reads from the piece of paper,
                  gesturing towards a cart loaded with presents*]

Esteban   I speak for Fuente Ovejuna, I start
                  By begging, from the bottom of my heart,
                  You to accept the presents in this cart.

                  Baskets shallow and baskets deep,
                  Blankets bright enough to make you weep,
                  A set of dinner plates painted with sheep.

                  Your courage the whole town celebrates
                  With strings of onions, boxes of dates
                  And oranges burning in their crates.

                  Preserved in brine you'll find delicate young
                  Piglets and calves – kidneys, brains, heart, lung
                  And there's our speciality – jellied tongue.

                  Sheepskins black and sheepskins white
                  And Mengo made this lamp – it shines as bright
                  As any angel. And it lasts all night.

                  We can't offer gold watches or works of art
                  Only the contents of this cart
                  And the golden love of the people's heart

                  And that's fine gold, and to show you how fine
                  Here are three hundred gallons of wine
                  To renew your courage whenever you dine

                  Your popularity is proved by these
                  Heart-felt tokens. Accept them, please.
                  And, may I recommend the local cheese?

[*Applause*]

Commander   I'd like to thank you and the town council.
[*To* SOLDIERS] Take the cart to my country house.

Alonso   Sir, you deserve a holiday.
You are welcome back to Fuente Ovejuna.
May the nearest tree to your house be struck by moonlight
And bear diamonds big as oranges.

Commander   Let's hope it does. I'll see you soon.

[*Exit* COMMANDER *into the door of the public building.* MUSICIANS
strike up and the PEOPLE *of Fuente Ovejuna, apart from* LAURENCIA
and PASCUALA, *march away with them*]

People of Fuente Ovejuna
[*Sing*]
Now he comes back to Fuente
For this is where his home is
We hope he stays for ever
Long live Commander Gomez!

[COMMANDER *looks out of the window of the public building*]

Commander   You two. Stay here.

Laurencia   What can we do for you, sir?

Commander   The other day you were rude to me
Just before I had to go
And risk my life on the battlefield.

Laurencia   Pascuala, were you rude to him?

Pascuala   I'm never rude to men, poor things.

Commander   You both insulted me.
Listen. Who rules this district?

Laurencia   The power's in your hands, Commander.

Commander   And therefore you are in my power. Correct?

Pascuala   Certainly, sir, politically speaking,
But not in any other sense.

Commander   I'd like a word with you both in here.
Plenty of people around, don't worry.

Laurencia   My father the Mayor will be back soon.
When he goes into the Council Offices
I will go in as well . . .

Commander	Captain Flores!
Flores	[*Appearing in the Square*] Sir!
Commander	What's wrong with these women? Why won't they do what they're told?
Flores	Come on, ladies, in we go.

[LAURENCIA *and* PASCUALA *fight off* FLORES *during the following exchanges*]

Laurencia	Keep your monkey claws off me.
Flores	Come on, ladies, let's be sensible.
Pascuala	Not a chance. You'd barricade us in with the Commander.
Flores	He only wants you to take a look At what he's brought back from the wars.
Commander	[*Appearing at window*] When they come in, lock the door behind 'em. [COMMANDER *disappears*]
Laurencia	Out of our way, Captain.

[*Enter* ORTUNO. *He joins in the struggle*]

Ortuno	Weren't you two presented to us Along with all the other rubbish on the cart?
Pascuala	I'll bite your bloody nose off.
Flores	Let 'em go. They're hopeless.
Laurencia	Isn't your Commander satisfied With all that wine and meat?
Ortuno	It's your meat he's after.
Laurencia	He'd choke on it.

[*Exit* LAURENCIA *and* PASCUALA]

Flores	How can we face him empty-handed? He'll curse us purple.
Ortuno	Part of the job, sir, if you can't take An officer's abuse Better quit the army and live as a beggar On fishbones and lemon juice.

[*Exit* FLORES *and* ORTUNO]

Scene 3

[*The Palace of* KING *Ferdinand and* QUEEN *Isabella.* KING, QUEEN, *Don* MANRIQUE *their minister, and their following enter*]

Queen   My lord, we must move straight away.
                  The King of Portugal's troops are poised to strike.
                  At any moment they may cut off your army.
                  Cuidad Real must be recaptured.

King   We can rely on Navarre and Aragon?

Queen   Of course.

King   I've been reorganising
                  My Castillian battalions.
                  We'll need them too.
                  Be patient, Isabella. We must think ahead.

Queen   Your majesty's convinced
                  That we have time for thinking?

Manrique   Your majesties, two aldermen
                  Escaped from the massacre at Cuidad Real.
                  They're here, begging to see you.

King   We'll see them now.

Manrique   You may come in.

                  [*Enter, travel-weary, two* ALDERMEN]

Queen   Let's hear your news.

First Alderman King Ferdinand, Queen Isabella,
                  Whom Heaven sent to help us.
                  We are humbly here from Cuidad Real
                  To plead for your protection.
                  Once we were proud and lucky men
                  Because we were your subjects.
                  But now we've lost that honour.

                  The Grand Master of Calatrava
                  Is greedy for more lands.
                  He is a lion of courage
                  Though a mere cub in years.
                  He laid siege to our city –
                  A most bitter siege.
                  All of us fought back so angrily
                  That every white-washed street

Was smeared with the blood of the dead.
In the end he conquered us
But he never could have done it
Without Commander Gomez
Who gave support, advice and soldiers.
Now the Grand Master rules Cuidad Real
And we're his sullen slaves.

King   Where are your fighting men?

Second Alderman

Some, sir, are prisoners.
And some are maimed and some are dead.
We have no other fighting men.

Queen   We must strike now.
We must, or the Portuguese
Will swarm all over our territories.

King   Don Manrique, march on Cuidad Real.
Take two companies with you.
Show no mercy to our enemies.

Manrique   I'll put an end to this boy's adventures
Or die in the attempt.

Queen   You will not die. I have no doubts at all.

King   Where is Commander Gomez now?

First Alderman   In Fuente Ovejuna, sire.
That's where he has his house
And what he calls his seat of justice.
And there he grabs, with his bony hand,
Their goods, their women and their land.

[*Exeunt* ALL]

Scene 4

[*A wood near Fuente Ovejuna. Enter* LAURENCIA *and* FRONDOSO]

Laurencia   Frondoso, you've made me climb all this way,
Leaving my washing half wrung out
Down by the stream. Sweet Jesus, what a climb,
And all so we can talk together
Without the town exploding with gossip.

You're such a trouble to me, Frondoso.
The town's talking anyway:
"He fancies her, you know", "She's after him".
Just because you're quick on your feet
And, some of my friends say, quite good-looking,
Well, not deformed, and just because
You're generally slightly better dressed
Than most of the shepherds on the hill
And just because you've not been elected
To be this year's village idiot –
There's not a boy or a girl in the whole of Fuente Ovejuna
Who's not certain as sin that we're lovers already
And they're simply counting the days until
Father Oliver stops playing his old bassoon
And mutters warnings to us from the pulpit.
They've decided how many children we'll have –
The whole business is out of control.

Frondoso   What do you feel about marrying me?

Laurencia   I don't feel much, one way or the other.

Frondoso   Please, Laurencia,
I'm in such a state,
I risk my life
Whenever I dare
Look into your eyes
Or listen to your voice.
You know I want to marry you
So why do you laugh at me?

Laurencia   I'm sorry, but little things make me laugh.

Frondoso   Aren't you upset that I'm so upset?
When I close my eyes, I see your face.
I can't sleep or eat or even drink.
How can an angel be so cruel?
God's honour, but you're driving me mad.

Laurencia   So go see a doctor, Frondoso.

Frondoso   You're the only doctor who can cure me.

Laurencia
We'll be like two doves
Gliding side by side
Over the mountains

Laurencia
We'll be like two doves
Perching on a branch
And cooing harmonies.

Laurencia   Have a quiet word with my uncle and my father.
It's not that I'm lovesick, but I'm beginning
To feel some of the symptoms.

Frondoso   Christ! It's the Commander.

Laurencia   He's out hunting deer.

Frondoso   Hide here.

Laurencia   There's no room. I'll hide over here.

[LAURENCIA *and* FRONDOSO *hide separately. Enter the* COMMANDER *carrying a crossbow. He spots* LAURENCIA *and grabs her wrist, dragging her into the open*]

Commander   Looks like my day.
I go out deer hunting
And catch a little doe.

Laurencia   I've just had a rest
After doing my washing.
I'll be off back down to the stream.
So good morning to you, Commander.

Commander   Shame that your manners aren't
As pretty as your face.
You're a peculiar creature, aren't you?
You've given me the slip
Several times in the town
But way out here –
In this lonely, secret wood,
Why, you're at bay, Laurencia,
You're trapped, Laurencia.
The only woman in Fuente Ovejuna
Too high and mighty to look in the eyes
Of her lord and master.
The other women like me, Laurencia,
Respectable married ladies and all.
You know Sebastiana?
Pedro Redondo's wife?
We did it together, Laurencia.
And Martin del Pozo's bride,

	What was her name? Just two days after she married him We did it together, Laurencia.
Laurencia	Yes, I do know those women, Commander. They've always been most generous To men of every kind. You know, if you weren't wearing that cross I'd take you for the devil himself. Go chase your deer and God be with you.

[COMMANDER *puts down his crossbow*]

Commander	I'm going to teach you a lesson, Laurencia, With my arms and with my hands And with my naked body.
Laurencia	You'd rape me? You're crazy!

[FRONDOSO *creeps out of hiding and takes the crossbow*]

Commander	It's no use. I've got you. Here. Come on.
Laurencia	Get off me, you bastard!
Commander	Come on. You want it, don't you? Come on. There's nobody here.

[FRONDOSO *pokes* COMMANDER *in the back with the crossbow*]

Frondoso	Let her go, Commander. Let her go or I'll be forced to Aim at the red cross on your chest And shoot your heart out.
Commander	Get out, you scruffy dog.
Frondoso	There's no dog here. Laurencia, run for it.
Laurencia	Be careful, Frondoso.
Frondoso	Run to your father's house.

[*Exit* LAURENCIA]

Commander	I put the crossbow down, you know. I didn't threaten her with it.
Frondoso	All I have to do Is press my finger – here – And you're a dead Commander.

Commander   She's got away. You know this is treason?
                     Lay down that crossbow, you bastard.

Frondoso   And let you shoot me?
                     I'm warning you – I love Laurencia –
                     And I'm as angry as a scorpion.

Commander   Oh I see, so a gentleman
                     Is expected to walk away
                     Offering his back as a target
                     To a mad young peasant?
                     All right, you son of a rat,
                     Shoot me – and then watch out for yourself.

Frondoso   Oh no, Commander, I don't shoot my betters.
                     I have this strange ambition
                     To become an old peasant one day.
                     So I think I'll take your crossbow away.

                     [*Exit* FRONDOSO]

Commander   To be insulted by a slave
                     And fall for a surprise attack!
                     I swear to God I'll pay him back
                     And I'll teach that little bitch how to behave
                     By screwing her on her sweetheart's grave.

                     [*End of Act One*]

Act 2

Scene 1

[*The Town Square.* ESTEBAN *and* ALONSO *sitting on bench*]

Esteban
We've got to think of the public good.
We mustn't draw on our reserve stocks of grain.
It looks like a bad year. Time to hang on
Whatever the rest of the council say.

Alonso
I'm with you. Caution's always been my policy.
That's why this town's such a peaceful place.

Esteban
We'll appeal to Commander Gomez about it.
We mustn't be fooled by these astrologers
Who know less than lizards about the weather
But try to convince us, with their turgid language,
They know secrets hidden from God himself.
They talk like bishops with hangovers. You've heard 'em:
"The past and the future form one great mystic circle".
All very fine, but if you ask
About something that matters here and now
Like where to lay drains or a sick donkey
They're about as much use as a woollen bucket.
Do you think, in their studies, there are stars and planets
And miniature galaxies whizzing around?
How else can they know what's happening in the skies
So they can peddle us their cheapjack prophecies?
While we're out sowing the fields,
They're indoors, doing their calculations:
Let's order a crop of so much wheat, barley, cereals,
So many tons of mustard, so many cucumbers –
Look, I've grown pumpkins with better brains on 'em.
The prophets announce: "A brown horse shall expire" –
And behold, it comes to pass – in Transylvania.
Or they tell us: "Lo, there shall be much beer
In Germany and verily behold
There will be cheese in Holland and rain in Scotland".
I'm not clairvoyant, but this I will say:
After April next year, with some luck, we'll have May.

[*Enter* LEONELO, *a student newly returned from the University of Salamanca, talking with* BARRILDO]

Leonelo	Enough, Barrildo, that's more than enough. I can't keep up with all the local gossip.
Barrildo	What's it like in Salamanca? How do they treat you at the University?
Leonelo	That's a long story.
Barrildo	You'll be very learned now?
Leonelo	I know a lot less than Pedro the barber And that's true of most of the other students.
Barrildo	Go on. They must have taught you a lot.
Leonelo	I'm beginning to learn what really matters.
Barrildo	Now they've started printing all these books The whole country's suddenly full of great thinkers.
Leonelo	So many books – and so much confusion! All around us an ocean of print And most of it covered in froth.
Barrildo	But books are good. Everyone knows, Leonelo.
Leonelo	You know that printing was invented In Germany by Gutenberg? So far so good. What happened then? All the most famous men in Europe Rushed into print, but once they were published Their ignorance was obvious to all. Next there arrived, like a swarm of fleas, The bawdy scribblers and the gallows hacks Writing any old cabbage for the sake of cash.
Barrildo	Leonelo, printing's essential.
Leonelo	We managed without it for thousands of years. In this great age of printing we haven't seen Any new author reach the heights Of Homer or Saint Augustine.
Barrildo	Leave it at that. Sit down. You're just being awkward. A holiday from thinking Is what you badly need. Whatever you say against printing I wish I was able to read.

[*Enter* JUAN ROJO *and another middle-aged* FARMER]

Juan Rojo	If you sold four farms and their stock You couldn't raise a dowry for your daughter, Not after the taxmen take their whack. You want to know why? The men who rule us Don't know there's any difference between Trying to grow corn out of dusty rock And selling necklaces in Madrid.
Farmer	What's the latest on the Commander?
Juan Rojo	Pesters the life out of my niece, Laurencia.
Farmer	What a shit! I'd like to see Him swinging from an olive tree.

[*Enter the* COMMANDER, FLORES *and* ORTUNO]

Commander	Another lovely evening, gentlemen?
Alonso	Sir.
Commander	Please – sit yourselves down.
Esteban	Commander – be seated wherever you like. We would prefer to stand.
Commander	But I'd prefer you to be seated.
Esteban	And I prefer to choose The company I keep.
Commander	Sit down, Chief Magistrate, I want a word with you.

[ESTEBAN *sits*]

Esteban	Did you see my greyhound racing yesterday?
Commander	No, but the Captain tells me It has an astonishing turn of speed.
Esteban	Yes, an incredible animal. You know, I think it can move as fast As a wanted criminal on the run Or the tongue of a coward under torture.
Commander	I'd like to take that greyhound of yours And set it on the trail of a hare Which keeps eluding me.
Esteban	Of course. And where's this hare?
Commander	In your daughter's shoes.

Esteban	My daughter?
Commander	Yes.
Esteban	The daughter of a small-town Mayor . . . Surely she's not good enough For a Commander?
Commander	You'd better teach her the way of the world.
Esteban	What do you mean?
Commander	She's been upsetting me. You see that woman – over there – Looks cold and snobbish, doesn't she? I scribbled her a little note. She was warming up my bed Before the ink was dry.
Esteban	If she did, she shouldn't have, And neither should you boast about it.
Commander	A preaching peasant! Captain Flores, Please order for Senor Esteban A copy of Aristotle on Politics. He needs it.
Esteban	Sir, here in Fuente Ovejuna We like the quiet life. We're good citizens, we pay our taxes And you should treat us with respect.
Leonelo	It's outrageous.
Commander	Oh dear, have I said something That's upset you, boy?
Leonelo	You mustn't talk to us like that. It's not right for you to insult The honour of our town.
Commander	Oh, you have honour, do you? Are you my brothers in arms In the great Order of Calatrava?
Leonelo	Some wearers of the Cross of Calatrava May be less honourable than cattle.
Commander	And am I dirtying the muck of your cowshed By walking through it, boy?
Leonelo	You're not making it any cleaner.

[COMMANDER *strikes* LEONELO. ORTUNO *restrains* LEONELO]

Commander   Is that so? Well, I'm honouring your cows by serving them.
Now get your slimy face out of my town.
If you ever come back I promise you
An interesting death.

Leonelo   You'll –

Commander   Out of my town!

[ORTUNO *forces* LEONELO *out of the Square and off*]

Esteban   Commander, you dishonour yourself.

Commander   These yokels are pathetic.
Life in the cities is so much freer –
No-one stops a man having his fun
So long as he's a gentleman.
City husbands are perfectly happy
For their wives to entertain me.

Esteban   No they're not. You want us to ignore
What's going on under our noses.
There is still such a thing as love in this town.
There is still such a thing as jealousy.
There is still such a thing as brutal lust.
There is still such a thing as sudden revenge.

Commander   [*To* SOLDIERS] Clear the Square!
[*To* TOWNSPEOPLE] Get out of here!

Esteban   You mean just us two,
Or the entire population of the town?

Commander   Out of this square!
Everybody out of this square!

Esteban   Don't worry, we're going.

Commander   Not in a mob like that! Disperse them!

Flores   Easy does it, sir.

Commander   These peasants imagine
They can gang up on me
As soon as my back's turned.

Ortuno   [*Returning*]
I think it's best if we all keep calm.

Commander   I'm absolutely calm.
Back to your nasty little homes!

[*Exuent all the* TOWNSPEOPLE]

Commander   Back to their holes, like mice.

Ortuno   Don't hide your feelings do you sir?

Commander   What d'you mean, Sergeant?

Ortuno   You don't like 'em not liking you.

Commander   I don't give a damn —
But they fancy they're as good as me.

Flores   Not really, sir.

Commander   What about that damn peasant?
Are you going to let him keep my crossbow?

Flores   Last night we had him cornered
Outside Laurencia's door.

Ortuno   I tripped him up,
Gave him a good kicking.

Flores   I started to whip him, then I saw
It wasn't the right peasant.

Ortuno   Had the same build.

Flores   All look alike.

Ortuno   Must've taught him something.

Commander   Where's this damned Frondoso?

Flores   The word is that he's still around.

Commander   Tries to kill me — and he's still around?

Ortuno   Fish are attracted magically
Towards the wriggling bait.
All an angler has to do
Is hold his rod and wait.

Commander   A shepherd threatens a Commander!
Flores, what's the world coming to?

Flores   Love causes all the trouble.

Ortuno   And the lover's still alive.

Commander   I'm a very patient man, Sergeant,
Otherwise I'd have taken my sword
And carved Laurencia's name
All over his stupid body.

But I've been trained to hold myself back
Till the best moment for an attack.
[*Consults a list*]
Well, I'll take Pascuala.

Flores   Pascuala's very sorry –
Says she's getting married.

Commander   I've no objection to that.

Flores   To tell you the truth, I think she's dead scared –
But we'll talk her round to it eventually.

Commander   What about Olalla?

Ortuno   That one likes a laugh.

Commander   Yes, she's a lively little creature.
What does Olalla say?

Ortuno   Her brand-new husband hides her away
Like wheat inside a bin
But she says as soon as she can get out
You shall be first man in.

Commander   Well done, Ortuno!
But her husband's watching her.

Ortuno   And he's got a temper
Like a rhinoceros with gout.

Commander   And Ines?

Flores   Which Ines?

Commander   Ines with the – you know – Anton's wife.

Flores   Pop round any day
Between nine and four
Please bring a bottle
Use the back door.

Commander   She's not much better
Than a marketday whore.
If only women
Esteemed themselves more.

Flores   There's nothing sweeter than the pain
Of delayed satisfaction.
If they give in too easily you miss
Drinking the wine of anticipation
Which makes us stagger with love.

Commander	When I get all worked up It's great if they give in. But how can you value a woman much If she opens up at the very first touch?

[*Enter* CIMBRANOS, *a messenger*]

Cimbranos	Where's the Commander?
Ortuno	Use your eyes.
Cimbranos	O brave Commander Gomez, Put on your white-plumed helmet and bright armour. Cuidad Real, won with so much blood and pain, Is in the greatest danger. All round its walls they're closing in Lit by a thousand smoky torches, The Master of Calatrava is at bay. Mount your horse now, sir, for the sight of you Will rout our enemies and save our Master.
Commander	Enough. Ortuno, have the bugle sounded. How many horsemen do I have?
Ortuno	Fifty-four, sir.
Commander	Tell them to mount and join me.
Cimbranos	They must be quick or Cuidad Real will fall To Ferdinand and Isabella.
Commander	Have no fear of that.

[EXEUNT]

[*Enter* LAURENCIA, MENGO *and* PASCUALA, *running*]

Pascuala	Stay with us, Mengo. The Commander's out to get us.
Mengo	What can I do?
Laurencia	The more we stay together The harder things are for the Commander.
Mengo	He's a devil.
Laurencia	He's a curse on the town.
Mengo	God send a thunderbolt And split him down the middle.

Laurencia	He's worse than arsenic and the Black Death Rolled into one.
Mengo	Is it true that Frondoso, out in the woods, Pointed a crossbow at his chest So you could run away?
Laurencia	I used to hate all men, But that moment changed my mind. I'm scared they'll kill him for it.
Mengo	Well he'd better get out of Fuente Ovejuna.
Laurencia	I tell him that, although I love him. But it makes him angry. He insists on staying And the Commander has sworn To string him up by one foot And then skin him alive.
Pascuala	That Commander needs strangling.
Mengo	Stoning would be better. I use a sling to guard my sheep. You can bet your boots That, if I let fly at him with a stone, The leather thong would no sooner creak Than his forehead would burst open like an egg.

[*Enter* JACINTA, *running*]

Jacinta	Jesus Christ, help me!
Laurencia	Jacinta! What's the matter?
Jacinta	Some of the Commander's men Broke down our front door with clubs. They said the Commander wanted me. They're after me now.
Laurencia	We'd all better hide. God help you Jacinta.

[*Exit* LAURENCIA]

Pascuala	He's after both of us as well.

[*Exit* PASCUALA]

Mengo	Men are supposed to fight, I suppose. Well, I've got a man's name and a man's body. Jacinta, stand behind me.

Jacinta	If only we had a gun.
Mengo	We'll have to use stones.

[MENGO *produces his sling. Enter* FLORES *and* ORTUNO]

Flores	I see – you thought you'd run away?
Jacinta	Mengo – it's them.
Mengo	Excuse me, sir. These poor country girls . . .
Ortuno	What's this then? Are you standing up for her?
Mengo	Well, I'll stand up with words. Sir, I'm Jacinta's cousin, so I must Protect her if I can.
Flores	Get him, Sergeant.
Mengo	Listen, if I lose my temper And let fly with my slingshot You'll bleed enough to fill a horse trough.

[*Enter* COMMANDER *and* CIMBRANOS]

Commander	Must I dismount to deal with brawlers?
Flores	One of the peasants from this filthy town Which you should have burned down long ago In my humble opinion, sir. He was obstructing us, disobeying orders And finally threatening us.
Mengo	Commander, sir, if you care about justice, You ought to punish these soldiers of yours. They've tried to carry off a country girl From her own parents' home. Please let me take her back to them.
Commander	I'll let my men Take their revenge on you. Drop that sling.
Mengo	[*Doing so*] Sir!
Commander	Flores. Ortuno. Cimbranos. Use it to tie his hands together.

Mengo	Is this the way you defend the peace?
Commander	Tell me, lad, What do the peasants of Fuente Ovejuna say about me?
Mengo	Sir, how have I offended you. How has Fuente Ovejuna offended you?
Flores	Shall we kill him, sir?
Commander	Don't waste your bullets. You'll need them at Cuidad Real.
Ortuno	What shall we do with him?
Commander	Tie him to that oak tree. Strip him naked. Use your horse's reins And whip him –
Mengo	Mercy!
Commander	Whip him until his back Is one dripping pattern of bright red and dark red.
Mengo	God!

[*Exit* FLORES, ORTUNO *and* CIMBRANOS *with* MENGO]

Commander	Jacinta, why were you running away?
Jacinta	Give me back to my father and mother!
Commander	You're safe with me, Jacinta. I belong to an order of chivalry.
Jacinta	My father is an honest man. You're far more rich and powerful And your parents may be aristocrats, But my father is much better than you – He always acts in an honourable way.
Commander	Jacinta, you're being insolent. That's not the way to pacify A soldier when he's angry. Over there with you. I'll give it to you here and now.

[*Sounds of whipping and* MENGO's *cries offstage*]

Jacinta	Watch what you're doing.

[JACINTA *fights off the* COMMANDER, *scratching his face*]

Commander	All right, Jacinta, I understand. You'll be pleased to know I don't want you now. I'll hand you over to my troops – They'll queue up and screw you one by one.
Jacinta	I'll kill myself.
Commander	You'll love it, peasant.
Jacinta	Please, Commander, show some mercy.
Commander	I don't have any of that stuff.
Jacinta	God will take his revenge on you.
Commander	That's up to him.

[*Exit* COMMANDER *forcing* JACINTA *before him, her arm twisted behind her*]

[*Enter* LAURENCIA *and* FRONDOSO]

Laurencia	My love, please, it's too dangerous.
Frondoso	I love you completely. I had to tell you. I saw you in the square And I wasn't scared any more.
Laurencia	The Commander –
Frondoso	Let's hope the people of Cuidad Real Finish off that bastard.
Laurencia	Don't say that. They say when you wish a man should die He usually lives to be A great-great grandfather.
Frondoso	Then I hope he lives a thousand painful years – And that takes care of him. Laurencia – I have to know – How do you feel about me and my love? You know how the town talks about us? They always couple our names together – Frondoso-Laurencia, Laurencia-Frondoso – And they wonder why we aren't coupling too. Darling is it yes or no?

Laurencia	I think there's only one of us.
Frondoso	Kiss me Laurencia. [*They kiss*] I feel as if I've just been born.
Laurencia	No time for speeches. Go talk with my father, That's the important thing. There he is, strolling with my uncle. Don't worry, they'll be for the marriage.
Frondoso	God help me, I hope so. [LAURENCIA *moves out of sight, but within hearing. Enter* ESTEBAN *with* ALONSO]
Esteban	The way he behaved . . . There was nearly a riot. He's just a bully. Everyone was shocked. And as for poor Jacinta . . .
Alonso	A terrible thing. Such a gentle girl.
Esteban	And poor old Mengo beaten.
Alonso	They whipped him raw. Disgraceful.
Esteban	And we're the Council. But what's the point of having a Council When he kicks us all around like this? I heard that just the other day He caught Pedro Redondo's wife Down by the waterside And when he'd finished with her He gave her to his Captain Who took his turn, then passed her to the Sergeant,
Alonso	Just a moment. Who's that?
Frondoso	Only me. Can I have a word?
Alonso	Of course, Frondoso, You're my favourite nephew.
Frondoso	Well, I want to ask you a favour, sir.
Esteban	Has that Commander Gomez Given you trouble?

Frondoso   All kinds of trouble.

Esteban   I thought as much.

Frondoso   The love you show me gives me the courage
                 To tell you this: I love Laurencia.
                 I want to marry her.
                 I'm sorry if you think this is too abrupt,
                 Blurting it out like this —

Esteban   Not at all, Frondoso, your timing is perfect.
                 There's been a splinter of dread in my heart
                 But you've removed it and saved my life.
                 I'm grateful to God for your love for Laurencia.
                 I have always been a lucky man.

Alonso   Shouldn't you ask Laurencia first?

Esteban   Don't worry your head about that, Alonso.
                 Laurencia must have said yes
                 Or he wouldn't have dared to ask me.
                 Let's settle the question of the dowry.
                 Gold coins, I thought.

Frondoso   I don't need any dowry.

Alonso   You're a lucky man, Esteban,
                 He'll take her as nature made her.

Esteban   I'll see what she has to say about dowries.

Alonso   That'd be just as well.

Frondoso   Certainly. I don't want
                 To trample on anyone's feelings,
                 Particularly hers.

Esteban   Daughter! Laurencia!

                 [*Enter* LAURENCIA]

Esteban   What an obedient daughter!
                 I call and she appears.

Laurencia   I was shopping at the fruit-stall.

Esteban   Laurencia,
                 I have been asked for your opinion.
                 Come over here please.
                 D'you think it's a good idea

	For Frondoso here to get married
	To your curly-haired friend Gila?
	He is the most intelligent young man
	In Fuente Ovejuna –

Laurencia   Gila's getting married?
To Frondoso?

Esteban   D'you think she's good enough for him?

Laurencia   Too good if anything.

Esteban   Very generous. But I don't agree.
Frondoso could do better for himself.
He might, for instance, marry you.

Laurencia   You will have your awful little joke, won't you?
Even at your age.

Esteban   Do you want this boy?

Laurencia   I've always liked him.
He's always liked me.
I was biding my time.
But now, because of you know who –

Esteban   Shall I say yes?

Laurencia   You say it for me, sir.

Esteban   Consider it said.

Alonso   Come, let's go look
For Frondoso's father.

Esteban   My son, about the dowry.
It'll be in gold.

Frondoso   I'd rather not, sir,
I'd be insulted.

Esteban   Swallow that insult, or you'll find instead
You're swallowing crusts of mouldy bread.

[*Exit* ESTEBAN *and* ALONSO]

Laurencia   Tell me, Frondoso, are you happy?

Frondoso   I'm too happy to say anything at all.

[*Exit* LAURENCIA *and* FRONDOSO]

Scene 2

[*Outside the city of Cuidad Real. A battle raging off-stage*]

[*Enter the* MASTER *of Calatrava,* COMMANDER *Gomez,* FLORES *and* ORTUNO]

Commander	Only one thing to do now, sir — take flight.
Master	The city walls were flimsy. Our enemies are mighty.
Commander	It's cost them more men than they can count.
Master	But they will never boast of winning The standard of Calatrava.
Commander	All your ambitions, Master, Trampled in the mud.
Master	What could I do? Fortune decides. One day she lifts you to the throne; Next day, down to the dungeons.
Voices	[*Off*] Ferdinand and Isabella! Victory! Victory! Ferdinand and Isabella!
Master	They're lighting beacons on the battlements. Down from the windows of high towers Their banners unroll like the tongues of dragons.
Commander	An expensive celebration — paid for in blood.
Master	Fernando Gomez, I shall return to Calatrava.
Commander	And I'll go back to Fuente Ovejuna. You must make up your own mind Whether to fight on in this cause Or bow your knee to Ferdinand and Isabella.
Master	I'll write to you about these matters.
Commander	Time will advise you.
Master	I am still young. I can't tell what will be. But time's already tricked me cruelly.

[*Exeunt*]

Scene 3

[*The Town Square in Fuente Ovejuna. The square is decorated
for the celebration of a wedding. Music. Enter the wedding
party for* LAURENCIA *and* FRONDOSO. MUSICIANS, MENGO, FRONDOSO,
LAURENCIA, PASCUALA, BARRILDO, ESTEBAN, JUAN ROJO, ALONSO, *the priest*
FATHER *Oliver etc. Villagers launch into a mocking song in which
individuals improvise alternate lines to answer chorus lines*]

All   [*Sing*]
                   Viva! Viva! The newly-weds!
                   May they never sleep in different beds.
                   Viva! Viva! The happy pair!
                   Twenty-one children may they bear.
                   Viva! Viva! The happy bride!
                   She's not the one who is terrified!
                   Viva! Viva! The happy groom!
                   May his little pistol go boom boom boom.
                   Viva Laurencia!
                   Viva Frondoso!
                   Viva Laurencia!
                   Viva Frondoso!

                   [ALL *dance*]

Mengo   What a lot of dog-eared doggerel.

Barrildo   I'd like to see you make up a better song.

Frondoso   Mengo knows more about whips than he does about song-
                   making.

Mengo   Just to wipe that grin off your face Frondoso,
                   Let me tell you this.
                   I know a man lives down the valley –
                   The Commander took him –

Barrildo   – Shut up, Mengo.
                   Just hearing the name of that butcher
                   Puts a blight on the day.

Mengo   One hundred strokes they gave me
                   For lawful possession of a slingshot.
                   But this man down the valley –
                   The Commander had him given
                   An enema of purple dye and pebbles.
                   I won't say the man's name

But he's highly respected by everyone.
How can we live with that sort of thing?

Barrildo   It's 'the Commander's idea of a joke.

Mengo   Enemas are no laughing matter.

Frondoso   Come on, Mengo, give us the song
You made up for our wedding.

Mengo   [*Sings*]
I wish the bride and bridegroom
May live a cheerful life
And never hit each other
With frying pan or knife

May they have many children
And lots of meat and wine
And may they live forever
Or till they're ninety-nine

This is the song of Mengo
For two of his best friends
I do hope they'll be happy
And so my ditty ends.

[LAURENCIA *kisses* MENGO]

Frondoso   If you're a poet, I'm the Pope.

Barrildo   And he made it up as he went along!

Mengo   I'm so glad you like it. I'll do you another.
A song about cooking fritters.

[*Sings*]
Have you seen a fritter fryer
When he's frying fritters?
The fat in the frying pan,
The pan upon the fire.
The fritter fryer takes some batter
When the fat is fizzing,
He flings it in the frying pan
And blows the fire higher.

When the fritter fryer takes the
Fritters from the fryer,
They're different shapes and sizes –
Like a squid or like a ball.
There's pretty ones and ugly ones and

Some are quite disgusting
They're frizzled to a frazzle
Or they're hardly fried at all.

That's how I think of poets
Making up their verses.
Their batter is their matter
And the paper is their pan.
There's pretty ones and ugly ones and
Some are quite revolting,
And nobody can swallow them
Unless the poet can!

Barrildo   That's enough clowning.
Silence for the bride!

Laurencia   I'm going to kiss you all.

[*Applause*]

Esteban   Please God
Give my daughter and her husband
A life as beautiful
As a deep lake in autumn time
Reflecting golden trees.

Frondoso   To us and all of you as well.

[*Applause*]

Father Oliver   Now they are man and wife –
Give us more music!

Barrildo   [*Sings*]
There was a maiden from the hill
Went walking by the stream
There came a knight from far away
He followed in a dream

She hid herself among the leaves
For she was young and shy
He sought her down the waterside
And he began to cry:

"Why do you hide yourself from me
O fairest of them all?
My love is long, my love is strong
And it breaks down every wall."

His sword it cut through bush and briar
Towards her hiding place.
She drew a branch in front of her
To hide her lily face.

But when he pulled that branch away
A bright snake did appear.
The snake did bite that lusty knight
And whispered in his ear:

"Why do you hide yourself from me,
O fairest of them all?
My love is long, my love is strong
And it breaks down every wall."

[*Enter* COMMANDER, FLORES, ORTUNO *and* SOLDIERS]

Commander	Please don't stop the celebrations – Not on my account.
Juan Rojo	We are happy to obey you, sir, in this. Perhaps you'd care to join our party? How did your battle go? Did you win? But what a question!
Frondoso	I'm as good as dead.
Laurencia	Frondoso – run!
Commander	Oh no. Arrest him. Tie his hands.
Juan Rojo	Give yourself up, lad.
Frondoso	You want to see me killed?
Juan Rojo	What do you mean?

[SOLDIERS *seize and bind* FRONDOSO]

Commander	I'm not the kind of soldier Who shoots down unarmed peasants. If I was these men of mine Would've skewered this hooligan by now. He goes to jail – and his father-in-law Can sit in judgement on him. Take him away.

[SOLDIERS *drag off* FRONDOSO]

Pascuala	But Commander, what's he done?

Commander He stole my crossbow.
Tried to murder me.

Pascuala Sir, he's just getting married.

Commander Fancy that, he's just getting married.
There are plenty of other louts in the town
The bride can marry instead.

Pascuala Please be generous, Commander.
Let him off this time.

Commander Pascuala, it's not up to me.
His offence was against the Order which I serve
And against the Grand Master, God protect him.
This man must be punished as an example
Or Fuente Ovejuna will breed more rebels.
He pointed a crossbow at my chest.

Esteban I'm his father-in-law.
Let me try to excuse him.
It's not amazing that a man who's a lover
Should occasionally forget himself.
You tried to take his wife away.
Wasn't it natural to defend her?

Commander Esteban — you're an idiot.

Esteban For your reputation's sake —

Commander — I never tried to take his wife.
The boy wasn't even married.

Esteban Yes, you did. Don't argue with me.
In Castile now a King and Queen
Are bringing peace to all the people
And stamping out petty tyrants.
When they have won the last of their battles
They will do well to cut down any man
Who preys upon the helpless.
Let King Ferdinand wear the red cross
For that insignia was made
Only for noble breasts.

Commander Remove his chain of office.

Esteban [*Handing it over*]
Take it, sir, you're welcome.

Commander   [*To* FLORES *and* ORTUNO]
Use this chain. Beat the magistrate.
The way I do when I break a horse.

Esteban   You are our overlord. Do what you like.

Pascuala   You'd beat an old man?

Laurencia   You only beat him because he's my father.
Why him? Why not me?

Commander   Later perhaps. Take them both away.
I want a guard of ten soldiers on them.

[*Exit* COMMANDER *and* SOLDIERS *with* ESTEBAN *and* LAURENCIA *under arrest*]

Pascuala   The wedding's turned into a funeral.

[*Exit* PASCUALA]

Barrildo   Is nobody man enough to stand up to him?

Mengo   I've had one whipping already.
My bruises are still ripe.

Barrildo   Let's all speak out together.

Mengo   Let's all keep quiet. They have the weapons.
I can still hear that leather crack
And I look like a raw steak from the back.

[*End of Act 2*]

Act 3

Scene 1

[*A modest meeting room. A hot day. Enter* ESTEBAN, ALONSO *and* BARRILDO]

Esteban   Just look who's turned up for the meeting!

Barrildo   Nobody.

Esteban   Pathetic.

Barrildo   Everybody in town was told.

Esteban   Frondoso chained up in the jail.
Leonelo thrown out of town.
Laurencia taken God knows where.
Great God Almighty!

Barrildo   And they beat you too.

[*Enter* JUAN ROJO *and a* FARMER]

Juan Rojo   Keep your voices down.
It's meant to be a secret meeting.

Esteban   It's a wonder we're not screaming.

[*Enter* MENGO]

Mengo   Is this the secret meeting?

Esteban   Sit down, Mengo.
Fellow citizens,
I speak as an old man
So pardon an old man's tears.
We ought to be in mourning
For the honour of our beloved town.
Which has been nailed into its coffin
And stuck in the cold depths of the earth.
How can we go on living, when all of us
Have been insulted by this thug?
Tell me, is there one man here
Whose life he hasn't wrecked?
You see, it's a disaster.

Juan Rojo   Worse than an earthquake.

Esteban	But who can help us?
Juan Rojo	King Ferdinand and Queen Isabella Have turned Cordoba into a peaceful place. Let's send two council members To ask them to save us.
Barrildo	King Ferdinand's too busy fighting battles To worry about Fuente Ovejuna.
Farmer	If anyone wants to know what I think, I think we should abandon the town, That's what I think.
Alonso	They steal our wives and daughters. They treat us like slaves.
Juan Rojo	So what can the town do?
Alonso	Kill these soldiers before they kill us. There's plenty of us – not many of them.
Mengo	They can always get more. We can't.
Barrildo	Let's share out the few weapons we have – and fight!
Esteban	God and the King and Queen – they're our only rulers – Not these strutting military men. What have we got to lose?
Mengo	Now just a moment, sir, hang on. Let's show a little caution, shall we? I represent the ordinary shepherd And he's always the one who comes off worst When important people fight it out. I would suggest that we wait and see – Speaking on behalf of the ordinary shepherd, that is.

[*Enter* LAURENCIA, *dishevelled*]

Laurencia	Out of my way and let me in To this all-wise, all-male Council meeting. You may not allow a woman to vote But you can't stop her yelling. Don't you know me, for God's sake?
Esteban	Yes, you're my daughter.
Juan Rojo	Laurencia!

Laurencia	Hard to recognise me, isn't it, The state I'm in?
Esteban	My daughter!
Laurencia	Don't call me that.
Esteban	Why not?
Laurencia	For lots of good reasons – The chief ones are these: Because you let those soldiers take me Without lifting a finger. Because you left it to Frondoso To protect me when that's a father's job Till after the wedding night. For, even if you buy a diamond ring It isn't yours till it's on your finger. So why did Frondoso have to run The gauntlet of those vicious troops?
Esteban	They beat me too, you know, when I protested.
Laurencia	They did, yes, I'm sorry, yes they did, but these others – When the Commander took me off You stood and goggled like cowardly shepherds While the wolf ran off with your lamb. Oh, did they hold you back with swords? Well, they held me down with violent abuse, With violent threats, with violent hands, With every kind of violence So he could violate me.

Doesn't my hair tell its own story?
Can you see the blood on my skirt?
Can you see the bruises
Where they clutched me?
Where they hit me?
Can you see anything at all?

Call yourselves respected councillors?
Call yourselves my kinsmen?
Your guts should burst out of your bellies
To see Laurencia like this.

Fuente Ovejuna – the spring for sheep.
Sheep, that's all you are, a flock of sheep.
Sheepspring's the right name for this town.
Give me your weapons

You're a heap of stones,
A shelf of plaster idols,
A knot of cold-hearted snakes –
No, that's not fair on snakes –
A snake at least
Follows the hunters who steal its eggs
And lashes out, biting into their legs,
Injecting venom before they can reach
The safety of their saddles.

You gang of rabbits – stay down your holes!
Ancient cockerels, loafing round the dunghill
While other men screw your wives.
Give me your swords.
Take my sewing needles.

My God, do we women have to show you
How to smash those bastards
And wash yourself clean in a trough of their blood?

Stones! Rabbits! Sheep! Eunuchs!

Tomorrow we women will dress you up
In our best skirts and blouses.
We'll paint and powder you prettily
And lead you round the houses.

Listen, the Commander has made up his mind
To murder Frondoso at his headquarters.
There'll be no trial. There'll be no verdict.
And maybe his body will be found in the river.
And maybe his body will never be found.

And when the Commander takes the rest of you,
One by one, week by week, and strings you up
While your fellow-councillors hold secret meetings –
I'll be laughing my head off – little boys!
O when he's killed all the men of this town
Then the age of Amazons will return
And women will show the world what courage means.

Esteban	Laurencia, I won't swallow those insults. I'll go out alone to fight, even though An army of devils marches against me.
Juan Rojo	I'm scared, it's true. But I'll come too.
Alonso	Let's risk everything and die together.

Barrildo	Tie a rag to the top of a stick, Hold it high in the wind. We'll kill those monsters.
Juan Rojo	What sort of order shall we march in?
Mengo	Just kill 'em, don't worry about what order. Stamp along in a thumping great mob, All of the townspeople, all together.
Esteban	Take crossbows, lances, Kitchen knives, hammers –
Mengo	Slingshots?
Esteban	Anything that can cut or batter.
Mengo	Long live our lords The King and Queen, Ferdinand and Isabella!
All	Long live the King and Queen!
Mengo	Death to all traitors! Death to all tyrants!
All	Death to all traitors! Death to all tyrants!

[*Exit all but* LAURENCIA. *She goes to the window*]

Laurencia	When sheep march out to the attack It's terrible news for the wolf-pack. [*Shouts*] Women of Fuente Ovejuna! Come and win your good names back! Women of Fuente Ovejuna! Everyone of you is needed!

[*Enter* PASCUALA, JACINTA *and other* WOMEN]

Pascuala	What's up? What are you shouting about?
Laurencia	Don't you see the men are marching out To assassinate Commander Gomez? Men, young lads and little boys, All rushing out to finish him off. D'you think it's right for the men of the town To tackle this alone? They've suffered less Than any of us women.

Jacinta   What can we do?

Laurencia   Form up in ranks and take part in an action
                     Which will shake the world.
                     Jacinta, because of what they did to you,
                     You shall march at the head of our column.

Jacinta   They hurt you as much as me.

Laurencia   Pascuala, you be standard bearer.

Pascuala   Just give me a moment to hoist
                     The flag up on a pole.
                     I'll bear it proudly, just watch me.

Laurencia   No time for embroidering banners.
                     Hold up your shawls, let them flow in the wind.

Pascuala   We ought to elect a captain.

Laurencia   No.

Pascuala   Why not?

Laurencia   Because we can fight bravely enough
                     Without a leader telling us how to die.

Laurencia and the Women
                     [*March and sing*]

                     The hands of ladies and gentlemen
                     Are soft as Chinese silk.
                     The hands of ladies and gentlemen
                     Are white as purest milk.
                     But we're not ladies or gentlemen
                     And we're not soft or white,
                     For we are women with peasants' hands
                     And our hands can caress or fight.

                     For our hands fight the tough old soil
                     With hoe and spade and plough.
                     They light the fires and pour the oil
                     And they milk the goat and cow.

                     And our hands help old lives to end
                     And they help new lives to start.
                     And they show affection to our friends
                     And put courage in our lover's heart,
                     And put courage in our lover's heart.

The hands of ladies and gentlemen
Are soft as Chinese silk.
The hands of ladies and gentlemen
Are white as purest milk.
But we're not ladies or gentlemen
And we're not soft or white,
For we are women with peasants' hands
And our hands can caress or fight.

And our hands plant the corn you eat
And weave the clothes you wear,
And scrub the floors and cook the meat
And they comb the children's hair.

But if a wolf attacks our flocks
Our hands will take its life
With crossbows and with well-aimed rocks,
With a sickle and a carving knife,
With a sickle and a carving knife.

Oh the hands of ladies and gentlemen . . .

[LAURENCIA *and the* WOMEN *march out of sight*]

Scene 2

[*Inside the Commander's country house. Enter* FRONDOSO, *his hands bound, led by* FLORES *and* ORTUNO *and followed by the* COMMANDER]

Commander	String him up on the beam And then we'll have some fun with him.
Flores	Right you are, Commander.
Frondoso	They all call you Commander. I know a better name for you.

[COMMANDER *hits* FRONDOSO]

Commander	Rope over the beam, Haul him up backwards by the arms. Drop him a few times. And then we can begin.
Frondoso	I could've killed you that day.

[*Sounds of off-stage singing and marching*]

Flores	What's happening out there?

Ortuno	We're going to be interrupted.
	[*Looks out of the window*]
	They're breaking down the gates, sir.
Laurencia	[*Off*] Break it down! Tear it down! Burn it down!
Ortuno	It's a mutiny, sir. The whole damn town.
Commander	Rebelling against me?
Flores	They're armed. They're out for blood. The gates are down, sir.
Commander	Untie the lad. Frondoso, you've got to go And calm them down.
	[FLORES *unties* FRONDOSO]
Frondoso	I'll do what I can.
Commander	What's the problem? What's got into them?
Frondoso	Love.
	[*Exit* FRONDOSO]
Mengo	[*Off*] Long live Ferdinand and Isabella! Death to all traitors!
Flores	For Christ's sake, sir, Don't let them corner you.
Commander	There's guards outside. They'll never get in.
Flores	When people are pushed so far That they take up arms They don't give them up till they've tasted blood.
Commander	We'll shoot them down.
Ortuno	Too many of them, sir.
Frondoso	[*Off*] Long live Fuente Ovejuna!

Commander	They're mad. But I can cure them.
Flores	We're mad if we stay here.

[*Enter* TOWNSPEOPLE *including* ESTEBAN, JUAN ROJO, PASCUALA, LAURENCIA, JACINTA, MENGO, FRONDOSO, BARRILDO *etc, all armed with weapons and farming implements*]

Esteban	The tyrant and his apes! Long live Fuente Ovejuna! Death to all traitors!
Commander	Now just a minute . . .
Laurencia	We've no time to waste. We're here to put things right.
Commander	Just tell me your complaints. If I've made some mistakes, I'll do my utmost To make up for them – I just want to say –
Townspeople	Fuente Ovejuna! Fuente Ovejuna! Death to rapists! Death to traitors!
Commander	Listen to me! I'm talking to you. I'm the Commander of this district.
Laurencia	Our only commanders are the King and Queen.
Commander	Wait. Let me –
Townspeople	Fuente Ovejuna! Fuente Ovejuna! Death to the Commander!
Commander	I must appeal to the women of the town –
Laurencia	We're not women – we're soldiers now.
Pascuala	Come on, let's drink his blood.
Jacinta	Cut him up for mincemeat!
Pascuala	Blood and mincemeat!

[TOWNSPEOPLE *have closed in on the* COMMANDER, FLORES *and* ORTUNO]

Esteban	Try this, Commander!
Commander	You're killing me. Have pity, Esteban. Mercy!
Barrildo	Here's Captain Flores.
Mengo	Let him have it. He gave me two thousand lashes.

Frondoso	I won't be happy until he's dead.
Laurencia	Let me at him.
Pascuala	Easy now. Make sure they don't escape.
Barrildo	Don't give me prayers! Don't give me I'm so sorry! You're a toy soldier!
Laurencia	Pascuala, I'm going in for the kill. My knife's so thirsty that it's shaking.
Barrildo	I've found that Sergeant.
Frondoso	Carve him up.

[FLORES *breaks out of the mob,* MENGO *after him*]

Flores	Mengo, have mercy. I was under orders.
Mengo	It wasn't just my flogging. You pimped for the Commander.
Pascuala	Let him go, Mengo. The women want him.
Mengo	Take him, you're welcome.
Pascuala	I'll pay him for your whipping.
Mengo	Carry on.
Jacinta	Kill the bastard!
Flores	Torn to pieces by women!
Pascuala	Thought you liked women?
Jacinta	Cut his throat.
Flores	Ladies! Mercy!

[ORTUNO *breaks out of the mob, chased by* LAURENCIA]

Ortuno	It wasn't me. It wasn't me!
Laurencia	I know who you are. Down on your knees. Women, here's one more.
Pascuala	I'll kill him if it kills me.
Townspeople	Long live Fuente Ovejuna!

[TOWNSPEOPLE *kill* ORTUNO. FLORES, *badly wounded, manages to escape as* TOWNSPEOPLE *crowd round* COMMANDER's *corpse*]

Scene 3

[*The Palace of* FERDINAND *and* ISABELLA. *Enter* KING *Ferdinand,* QUEEN *Isabella and Don* MANRIQUE]

Manrique   We moved at the right time, your majesties.
We won the day with little opposition.
Now our forces occupy Cuidad Real
In case the enemy attacks again.

King   Well done. We shall send reinforcements.
That city commands the pass to Portugal.
We intend to hold it forever –
A bastion against the Portuguese.

[FLORES *is helped on, wounded*]

Flores   Your majesties. Bad news.
The worst atrocity.

Queen   Tell us.

Flores   Your majesty, my wounds.
I can't hold out much longer.
They brought me here from Fuente Ovejuna.
The people of that town, the men and the women,
Murdered Commander Gomez.
They worked themselves up
Over nothing at all –
Tore him to shreds, sir.
The whole damned town,
Fuente Ovejuna,
Shouting: Down with the tyrant!
Got so excited by their own shouting
They broke down their doors of his house
And in they burst
And they took no notice when he swore on his honour
To repay anything he owed them,
They took no notice and they struck him down,
Stabbing right through the red cross on his breast
With a thousand vicious gashes,
And they picked him up and sent him flying down
From a high window

And a mob of howling women underneath
Caught his body on the points of pitchforks,
Tossed him, caught him,
Tossed him, dropped him,
Dragged him into a barn.
They fought each other to pull out his hair,
Scratched his face to pieces with their nails.
It was hysteria, your majesties,
So bad that when they'd finished hacking him
The biggest pieces left were his two ears.
They burned his coat of arms.
They sacked his house and looted it.

I was mobbed too,
But managed to find a hiding place.
From there I watched and saw all this.
Later I escaped, was found by your soldiers
And brought here.

Your majesties, punish these barbarians.
The Commander's blood cries out for justice.

King   Captain Flores, you may rest assured
They will not go unpunished.
Don Manrique, I appoint you Judge.
Go find out all the facts of the case
And punish the offenders.

Queen   Send a strong troop of soldiers with the Judge.
He'll need protection in such a place.

King   Bind up this soldier's wounds and give
Him all your care —

Flores   — I do not want to live.

[*Exeunt*]

Scene 4

[*The Town Square at Fuente Ovejuna. Enter* TOWNSPEOPLE *and*
MUSICIANS *celebrating, with The Commander's head stuck on a pole*]

Townspeople   [*Sing*]
Have you seen our Commander
With his boots and medals on?
Have you seen our Commander?
No I think our Commander's gone.

Barrildo   Frondoso – sing your verse.

Frondoso   Here goes – and if you don't like it,
You make up a better one.

[*Sings*]

The first time I saw the Commander
He was strutting down the street.
The last time I saw the Commander
He looked like sausage-meat.

Townspeople   Have you seen our Commander
With his boots and medals on?
Have you seen our Commander?
No I think our Commander's gone.

Laurencia   Your turn, Barrildo.

Barrildo   Listen carefully.
Took a long time to compose this.

Pascuala   Well, sing it slowly then.

Barrildo   [*Sings*]
The first time I saw the Commander
He was courting someone's wife.
The last time I saw the Commander
He was pleading for his life.

Townspeople   Have you seen our Commander?
With his boots and medals on?
Have you seen our Commander?
No I think our Commander's gone.

Laurencia   Mengo's turn.

Frondoso   Come on, Mengo.

Mengo   My verse is very tasty.

Pascuala   Like tripe.

Mengo   The first time I saw the Commander
He was whipping me half-dead.
The last time I saw the Commander
The Commander lost his head.

Townspeople   Have you seen our Commander
With his boots and medals on?
Have you seen our Commander?
No I think the Commander's gone.

Esteban   Take his head away and give it decent burial.

Mengo	Yes, he's a miserable looking sod.

[ALONSO *brings out two glorious coats of arms*]

Pascuala	What are those for?
Alonso	They are the coats of arms of our true lords – King Ferdinand and Queen Isabella.
Esteban	Hang them here, each side of the Town Hall door.

[JUAN ROJO *brings out a simple plaque painted with a sheep
rampant and a fountain*]

Juan Rojo	And here's Fuente Ovejuna's coat of arms.
Frondoso	It's a fine piece of work. Who painted it?

[MENGO *tries to look modest*]

Laurencia	Hang it between the other two. A new day is dawning for Fuente Ovejuna.
Esteban	But it won't be long before the dark arrives.
Mengo	What do you mean?
Esteban	The King and Queen are sending a Judge. He and his investigators Will do anything to find out Who killed the Commander. We must all agree On what we're going to tell them.
Frondoso	What can we say?
Esteban	If they ask you who killed him And they put you to the torture Die saying "Fuente Ovejuna". Nobody budge from that.
Frondoso	And it's the truth – Fuente Ovejuna did kill the Commander.
Esteban	What will you say?
All	[*Raggedly*] Fuente Ovejuna.
Esteban	I'd better show you what I mean. Let's rehearse it. I'll be the torturer. Now who can be the one who's being questioned? Ah yes . . . Mengo!

Mengo	Couldn't you find someone feebler than me?
Esteban	Impossible. Come on, man. We'll only pretend to torture you.
Mengo	All right. Do your worst. Pretending.
Esteban	Mengo, who killed the Commander?
Mengo	Fuente Ovejuna did it.
Esteban	What if I torture you? Will you change your story?
Mengo	Not even if you kill me dead. It was Fuente Ovejuna.
Esteban	Confess, you scum.
Mengo	All right, I'll confess.
Esteban	Who did it then?
Mengo	Fuente Ovejuna.
Esteban	Tear out his nails.
Mengo	That's nothing. Fuente Ovejuna!

[*Enter* ALONSO, *agitated*]

Alonso	The Judge has arrived. With a troop of soldiers.
Esteban	Everyone, go to your homes.
Alonso	They're rounding up everyone.
Esteban	Don't be afraid. You all know what you have to say?
All	Yes!
Alonso	What's that?
Esteban	When we're asked who killed the Commander We say – Mengo, who killed the Commander?
Mengo	Fuente Ovejuna!

[*Enter* MANRIQUE *with* SOLDIERS]

Manrique	Ladies and gentlemen, Judgement has come to Fuente Ovejuna. I represent the King and Queen today And I am here to investigate the death of Commander Gomez de Guzman. I will conduct my interviews in the Town Hall And I want to talk with every one of you.

[*Exeunt*]

Scene 5

[*The* MASTER *of Calatrava's tent. The* MASTER *seated, a* SOLDIER *standing*]

Master	That was a terrible way to die. You, I shall have you killed For bringing me such news.
Soldier	I'm only the messenger, sir, I meant no harm.
Master	A town of savages! They dared do such a thing? Well, I shall take five hundred men And Fuente Ovejuna shall be burned. That town will be a black patch on the ground. I'll burn their bones and their children's bones.
Soldier	Control your anger, sir. The people of Fuente Ovejuna have declared their loyalty To Ferdinand and Isabella. You're on the wrong side of the King already.
Master	How can they declare for the King and Queen When the Order of Calatrava owns their town?
Soldier	You'll have to settle that with King Ferdinand. I suppose you could bring a law-suit against him.
Master	Idiot! How could I ever win? No, I'll bank down my anger And seek an audience with the King and Queen. I have been a rebel, but I may be pardoned By such a gracious Queen and King. Youth's an excuse for anything.

[*Exeunt*]

Scene 6

[*The Town Square.* FRONDOSO *and* LAURENCIA *stand and listen to the interrogations taking place off stage*]

Laurencia	My love, I'm terrified they'll kill you. For God's sake, get out of this town.
Frondoso	I'm not going to abandon my friends Just to save my own skin.

[*Screams from the hall*]

Laurencia   Listen. What's happening.

Manrique   [*Off*]
Come on, grandad, I want the truth.

Frondoso   They're torturing an old man.

Laurencia   Bastards.

Esteban   [*Off*]
Give me a minute's peace!

Manrique   [*Off*]
Slacken off a bit.
Tell me, who killed Commander Gomez?

Esteban   [*Off*]
Fuente Ovejuna did it.

Laurencia   God bless you, father.

Frondoso   He's a brave man.

Manrique   [*Off*]
Take that boy.
That's right.
I know you know who did it, you little pig.
You won't talk?
Tighten it!
Who killed him?

Boy   [*Off*]
Fuente Ovejuna, sir.

Manrique   [*Off*]
Peasants!
I'll hang the lot of you with my own two hands.
Who killed the Commander?

Frondoso   He's only a boy.

Boy   [*Off*]
Fuente Ovejuna!

Laurencia   It's a brave town.

Frondoso   Brave and strong.

Manrique   [*Off*]
Now that woman.
Hold her down.
Begin!

Laurencia	He's going mad.
Manrique	[*Off*] I'll skin you all alive. I'm warning you. Come on, who killed the Commander?
Pascuala	[*Off*] Fuente Ovejuna.
Manrique	[*Off*] Now! Show her what pain is!
Frondoso	Pascuala! She'll never hold out.
Laurencia	Pascuala won't break.
Manrique	[*Off*] I think they're enjoying it. Don't play games with me, girl. Let her have it.
Pascuala	[*Off*] Jesus Christ!
Manrique	[*Off*] I said let her have it! Are you deaf?
Pascuala	[*Off*] Fuente Ovejuna did it.
Manrique	[*Off*] I'll take the fat one next.
Laurencia	Poor old Mengo! That must be him.
Frondoso	Mengo! He's bound to crack.
Mengo	[*Off*] Oh! Oh!
Manrique	[*Off*] Turn it again.
Mengo	[*Off*] Oh!
Manrique	[*Off*] Tighter. Do I have to help you?

Mengo	[*Off*] Oh! Oh!
Manrique	[*Off*] Who killed the Commander?
Mengo	[*Off*] Stop! I'll tell you, sir.
Manrique	[*Off*] Slacken it off a little.
Frondoso	He's going to talk.
Manrique	[*Off*] Ready to start again?
Mengo	[*Off*] I know who killed him!
Manrique	[*Off*] Who?
Mengo	[*Off*] Fuente Ovejuna.
Manrique	[*Off*] A townful of idiots! They're laughing at the pain. I was sure I'd break that fat one down. Oh, let them go for the moment.

[*Enter* MENGO, ESTEBAN, PASCUALA *and* BOY, *with other* TOWNSPEOPLE]

Frondoso	Mengo! You're a hero.
Esteban	That's what I say too.
Mengo	Oh God!
Esteban	[*Producing a flask*] Have a drink, Mengo.
Mengo	[*Drinking and spluttering*] What is that stuff?
Esteban	Home-brewed brandy. Don't you like it?
Mengo	Oh God. Give me another go at it.
Frondoso	Must be good.
Esteban	Have another.
Mengo	Yes please.

Frondoso	You deserve it.
Laurencia	Put a blanket round him, he's shivering.
Esteban	Want some more?
Mengo	Well, just a few more.
Pascuala	Pass it round, we all need a drink. [*Drinks*] Oh good Lord above.
Laurencia	What's the matter?
Pascuala	It's a bit rough. [*Takes another swig*]
Frondoso	[*Producing another flask*] Here, try mine. Mengo, who killed the Commander?
Mengo	Fuente Ovejuna did it.

[*Exit all but* LAURENCIA *and* FRONDOSO]

Frondoso	Tell me, my love, now we're all alone . . . Who did kill the Commander?
Laurencia	Fuente Ovejuna, my darling.
Frondoso	Who killed him?
Laurencia	Frondoso, I'm scared. Well, it was Fuente Ovejuna.
Frondoso	And me, what do I kill you with?
Laurencia	What with? With loving you so much.

[*Exit* LAURENCIA *and* FRONDOSO]

Scene 7

[*The Palace of* KING *Ferdinand and* QUEEN *Isabella. Enter* KING *and* QUEEN, *meeting*]

Queen	How lucky I am, my lord, To welcome you home again To your palace and my arms.
King	My eyes are stinging with the dust Which rises from the yellow roads – I look at you – my eyes feel young again. But tell me, what is happening in Castile?

Queen	Castile is peaceful once again, Orderly, in control.
King	Hardly surprising, under your rule, my lady.

[*Enter* CIMBRANOS]

Cimbranos	The Master of Calatrava Implores you to grant him an audience.
Queen	I've heard so much talk about the boy That I'm fascinated to see what he's like.
King	He's a very young man – They're all much the same.
Cimbranos	He has fought bravely in two battles And he has aged considerably.

[*Exit* CIMBRANOS. *Enter the* MASTER *of Calatrava. He kneels*]

Master The Master of Calatrava
Most humbly begs your royal forgiveness.

I was wrong, I was deceived.
I struggled against you and I stole from you –
And all because I am so young.
The bad advice of Commander Gomez
And my own vanity and self-interest
Sent me galloping headlong down a wicked road –
So I beg for your forgiveness.

And if you can forget my sins
I will engage from this day on
To serve you most wholeheartedly,
For I would ride along with you
To that great battleground to which you go
And there, in bright Granada, there I'll prove my courage.

My sword, the moment it's unsheathed
Will spread terror amongst your foes
And you shall see red crosses spring
From all Granada's battlements.
And furthermore,I'll bring with me
Five hundred soldiers and a vow
That I will serve you all my life.

King Rise, Master, from your knees.
You came to us bravely of your own accord,
So you are very welcome.

Master	You are the healer of the sick.
Queen	Your prowess in battle, I am told, Even excels your skill with words.
Master	You are as beautiful as Esther was And you, sir, merciful as Xerxes.

[*Enter* CIMBRANOS]

Cimbranos	Your majesties, your Judge Is back from Fuente Ovejuna.
King	[*To* QUEEN] You shall pass judgement on these rioters.
Master	It is, of course, your Majesty, your concern, But were it mine, I would teach them a lesson For killing their Commander.
King	It is no longer your concern.

[*Enter* MANRIQUE]

Manrique	Your majesties, I travelled to Fuente Ovejuna And, as you requested, Conducted my inquiry With care and diligence. However, in all the evidence I found We do not have one single page, No, not a single sentence written down Which names the perpetrator of this crime.
	The people of the town were stubborn. Whenever I asked the name of the murderer All they would say was: "Fuente Ovejuna".
	I interrogated three hundred of them. All the approved tortures, rigorously applied. Old men, women, ten year old boys, But I could get nothing out of them Except the cry of "Fuente Ovejuna".
Queen	But if it's impossible To find out who it was We'll either have to pardon them Or execute them all.
Manrique	They are all here.
King	Let them be brought before us.

[*Enter the* TOWNSPEOPLE *of Fuente Ovejuna, guarded*]

Laurencia   Is that the King and Queen?

Frondoso   The rulers of Castile and Aragon.

Laurencia   Oh, they are so beautiful.
St Anthony's blessings fall upon them!

Queen   Are these the barbarians, the murderers?

Esteban   Your majesties,
The town of Fuente Ovejuna stands before you.
A town which is loyal and longs to serve you.
The cruelty of the late Commander
Was the root of all our troubles.
He stole our farms. He raped our women.
He had no pity for anyone.

Frondoso   That's right.
This is the young woman
God sent me for a bride.
I was the luckiest man alive –

Laurencia   – But on our wedding night
The Commander and his men carried me off –

Frondoso   And she resisted and they hurt her –

Mengo   Permission, sir, to say a few words?
Permission, madam? Prepare yourselves
To be dumbfounded by my account
Of the behaviour of Fernando Gomez.

Because I tried to protect a young woman
From being abducted by his bullies,
That little Nero had me flogged
Till my back looked like a side of smoked salmon.
Three burly soldiers beat my drum
With such rhythmic energy
That I've had to spend my life savings on
Linament and myrtle powder.
I can prove all this, your majesties.
Would you care to inspect my scars?

King   Later, perhaps.

Esteban   Sir, we wish to live under your rule.
You are our rightful overlord.
My lady, we ask for your leniency

Hoping you'll understand
The innocence and courage of our town.

Queen   No written evidence exists
Naming the person who
Committed this most vicious crime –
So we must pardon you.

[*Cheers*]

King   Fuente Ovejuna, you turned to us for help,
Therefore your town shall be
Ruled by ourselves from this day on –
And we'll watch you carefully,
Till we can find a new Commander
Who's fit ti govern such a town
As Fuente Ovejuna.

Laurencia Your gracious majesties, we must
Thank you for being both kind and just
And it's on this happy note, good friends,
That the story of Fuente Ovejuna ends.

[*The End*]

Lost in a Mirror

(It Serves Them Right)

Act 1

Scene One

[*A street in Ferrara*]

[*Night. Enter the* DUKE OF FERRARA *and his two servants* RICARDO *and* FEBO. *All three wear animal masks – the* DUKE *has a fox mask,* RICARDO *a cat mask and* FEBO *a pig mask. But these should be the kind of forehead masks which leave the actors' faces clear*]

Ricardo	What a wonderful joke!
Febo	I think the Duke looks Just like a fox. Not like a Duke.
Duke	It's essential. I mustn't be recognised.
Ricardo	Don't worry, your Grace, when you're in disguise, Nothing's forbidden, anything goes, And it's night, so even the sky's disguised. Take a look at the sky With his mask of cloud And his starry sword. Watch him stalk by In his space-black cloak. He Will dance to love's tune On the tiles of the moon Till his dew falls to soak me.
Duke	Enough nonsense, you fool.
Febo	Sir, he'll feel better for Having a metaphor, He's of the fashionable school.
Ricardo	You don't like modern poetry? Please accept my apology, Lock me up in an anthology – Throw away the key.
Duke	I don't like verse based on pretence. I want reality and playfulness, A good story and seriousness – But you're all simile and no sense Like a magician who pops in his hat

Rabbits, watches, pigeons, robins –
And changes them all into – coloured ribbons!
One gets tired of ribbons after a bit.
All right, let's lock up the poetry shop.
Ricardo, I'd like you to bring to my bed
That curly-haired woman. She's not too bad.

Ricardo   Not too bad? She's an angel in human shape.
Unfortunately there's a danger –

Duke   – Danger adds spice to any affair –

Ricardo   – Yes? Well, her husband's built like a bear
And he's a notorious dog in the manger.

Febo   He's got a horrible, hairy red face.

Duke   I can't stand people who are mean;
But then, Ferrara's always been
A rather selfish sort of place.

Febo   If I get a wife, and some day I will,
And somebody gives her precious stones
And foreign perfumes and golden gowns –
I'll pity the fool who's footing the bill,
For, if that wife is to get ill
And sicken and die, do you know what?
I'll inherit the whole bloody lot
And that poor sucker gets nothing at all.

Ricardo   People as this husband of yours
Are about as charitable as the Alps.

Duke   Lickpenny wife-misers! Stingy whelps!
The Devil curse them with sticky sores!

Ricardo   Since you're in an eloquent mood
You might strike lucky at that window.

Duke   Whose is it?

Ricardo   A self righteous widow,
Blessed with two daughters.

Duke   Yes?

Ricardo   The one
Is round and simple, like a pearl
The other's a diamond of a girl.
Two green grapes ripening in the sun.

Duke   I don't judge by looks. They always let you down.

Ricardo	I know a woman, a real good-looker, Lives near the west gate of the town.
Duke	What's she like?
Ricardo	She's sweet and brown, Just like demerara sugar.
Duke	Has she got fire in her blood?
Ricardo	Burning brown sugar. She's kept by a fool Who's a morose, castrated bull –
Febo	All he can do is chew the cud.
Ricardo	Then there's this woman lives next door – There's a witty talker for yer, Yes, she could have been a lawyer If she'd had the time to study law.
Duke	Rattle your sword upon her shutter.
Ricardo	No, she won't open at this time.
Duke	Suppose I tell her who I am?
Ricardo	Of course, sir, that's a different matter.
Duke	Call to her then.
Ricardo	Look, she's awake, Roused by the scent of aristocracy.

[CINTIA *looks out of her window. She's a courtesan*]

Cintia	Who's that down there?
Febo	It's me.
Cintia	Who?
Ricardo	Me.
Cintia	Who the hell's me, for heaven's sake?
Ricardo	Friends. Open up and hurry up about it – The Duke's here. I gave such a gallant Estimation of you talent –
Cintia	The Duke of Ferrara?
Ricardo	Do you doubt it?
Cintia	I don't doubt that the Duke might be Out with you two, but I can Hardly believe such a great man Would condescend to call on me.

Ricardo	You're a lady. We're being discreet.
	That's why the Duke's in disguise, you know.
Cintia	If you told me this only a month ago
	I'd believe the Duke was in this street,
	In my house and even in my bed. Yes.
	Since that man was a child
	He has acted so wild
	That his name is a by-word for randiness.
	Why hasn't he married? Let me tell you –
	It's obvious that he didn't care
	That his bastard son was his only heir –
	He'd stay single and do what he wanted to do.
	(I believe Federico, his bastard son,
	Is a worthy young man. That's not the point, is it?)
	A month back the Duke might have paid me a visit –
	But haven't you heard what the Duke has done?
	He's reformed! I know, I laughed till I cried!
	And he's going to get married! It's true! There you are!
	And his son's been sent off to Mantua
	To fetch young Casandra, his promised bride.
	So the Duke's in his Palace, there's no doubt,
	He'll be preparing for the big day,
	Ordering banquets and so on. Anyway
	He's not in Ferrara, gadding about.
	Look there's one thing I can't abide –
	Disloyalty. It's a real shame
	To go round blackening your master's name
	When he's home and probably tucked up in bed.
	And I'm for bed too. Goodnight, Ferrara.
	I expect you invented a tale like that
	Just to inveigle me into a chat.
	Goodnight, gentlemen, come back tomorrow.
Duke	Ricardo, this is a fine bordello.
Ricardo	She's never been known to refuse before.
Duke	I don't ask much. Am I being unfair?
	I need a woman. Get one, fellow!
Febo	Shall I kick down her door?
Duke	You shouldn't drink.
Febo	It's Ricardo's fault, sir.
Duke	Is that so?

Febo	Sir, if a ruler would like to know What his subjects truly think, Whether he's loved or whether he's feared, Then let him shun the flattery Of those who wear his livery. Let him don a cloak and a false beard. Let him mix with the people on market days And, while pretending to do the shopping, Learn what they think of him by eavesdropping. (I've often seen Kings and Dukes do that in plays.)
Duke	Listen, Febo, if you were God And, disguised went round the market-place Asking: "What do you feel about God, please?" Nine out of ten would say nothing good. The people are not the repository Of any special truth. Their good opinion Is a fickle, treacherous companion. Their judgement is haphazard as may be. Some grumbler, some discontented ape, Frustrated by his wife or job, Throws a fat lie to the mob And the mob roars, and eats it up. Since they are of low degree The people can't enter palaces – So how can they know what the truth is? Yet they murmur against the nobility. I did not wed, for I didn't intend My title to go to anyone But Federico, my dear bastard son. Yet now I must marry, my wild times must end.
Febo	Well, marriage makyth man, they say.
Ricardo	Here's something to be grateful for! You Grace, place your ear against this door.
Duke	Is someone singing?
Febo	I can't quite see.
Duke	Who lives in there?
Ricardo	A jocular Actor-manager and company.
Febo	Yes, they're the best in Italy.
Duke	They sing well. But are they popular?

Ricardo	Between friends and enemies they have found:
	From their friends they get love and kisses,
	From their enemies, boos and hisses.
Febo	Nobody gets praise all round.
Duke	Febo, for our wedding feast
	Invite this company to stage
	The choicest dramas of our age.
	But nothing vulgar in the least.
Febo	We'll have some critical gentlemen see a
	Fine selection of plays. They'll guide
	My choice of plays for you and your bride.
	(My best friends are intelligensia.)
Ricardo	I can hear Andrelina. She's going to sing.
Duke	Andrelina? She's famous. I'm listening.
Andrelina	[*Sings, within:*]
	No more thinking,
	No more remembering,
	No more, never no more.
	I was happy
	Till I started thinking
	I was happy
	Till I remembered.
	Now I live in agony.
	No more thinking
	No more remembering,
	No more, never no more.
	I want nothing.
	I just want oblivion.
	I want nothing,
	That's all I long for –
	Want to lose my memory.
	No more thinking,
	No more remembering,
	No more, never no more.
Duke	A powerful song!
Febo	And well expressed.
Duke	I'd like to hear more. But I feel half-dead.
	I think I'll wander home to bed.

Ricardo	To bed on your own?
Duke	Yes, I'm depressed.
Ricardo	But Andrelina is unique.
Duke	Unique perhaps, and far too strong. My heart is battered by her song.
Ricardo	Too much truth? Is the truth so bleak?
Duke	Ricardo, watch a play carefully And it's a mirror in which we may see The idiot, the thinker and the old, The young, the cowardly, the bold. The King, servant, soldier and mayor, The maid, the married woman – all are there To act as models of how life can be And how to live it honourably. This mirror shows our goodness and our badness. It shines with jests, then clouds with sadness. There was a note in Andrelina's song Which made my heart howl that my life's gone wrong. And should I listen to that song again? No, I'll go home to nurse my inner pain.

[*Exeunt*]

Scene Two

[*A road near a river. Enter* FEDERICO *in smart travelling clothes, and his servant* BATIN. *Pronounced Bateen*]

Batin	I don't understand why you're lurking around. Leave these weeping willows to weep. Federico, you have an appointment to keep And it's urgent.
Federico	Disappointment slows me down. I have no taste for company. I want to brood, under this canopy Of trees which bow their loveliness To touch the rippled river's drowsiness. In this deep looking-glass the willows stare. Admiring the green gowns they wear. Wish I could fly, and leave myself behind. I'm tired of mulling over in my mind My father's marriage. I was to have been

His heir, but now – well, you have seen
How I pretend in public to be glad.
But, Batin, in my heart I'm deathly sad.
To Mantua, with a numbed mind, I ride.
I go to collect my father's bride.
I go to gather up poison for me.
I have the feeling that this has to be.

Batin   The lecherous things your father's done
Have been condemned by everyone,
But virtue wins in the end, of course,
Marry a rake, and cure a rampant horse.

[*Sings*]
There was a well-loved King of France
And all the world would bring
Precious presents to his court
To show they loved the King.
One day a wise man brought a gift
A horse that shone like snow
And the King of France was pleased
For how was he to know?

It was a horse, wild as the sea,
No man could ride upon.
It was a horse of ivory,
It was a horse called Swan.

And from its head down to its hoofs
There fell a milk-white mane
And the spirit of that horse
Was full of high disdain.
The bravest trainers in the land
Have tried with all their skill
But not one of them can break
That angry horse's will.

It was a horse, wild as the sea,
No man could ride upon.
It was a horse of ivory,
It was a horse called Swan

The King has put Swan in a cave,
A lion at its side,
And when the horse has seen the beast
Its soul has nearly died.
But now its curly mane stands up,

Each hair is like a spine
And that proud horse seems to be changed
To a white porcupine.

> It was a horse, wild as the sea,
> No man could ride upon.
> It was a horse of ivory,
> It was a horse called Swan.

And now the horse no man could break
Is courteous and mild,
And now the angry horse called Swan
Is ridden by a child.
And now the horse no man could break
A dwarf can ride upon.
And that is how the King of France
Has tamed a horse called Swan.

> It was a horse, wild as the sea,
> No man could ride upon.
> It was a horse of ivory,
> It was a horse called Swan.

Federico   Batin, I know that for my father's case
The usual cure is marriage.
But he promised me his estate
And now that proves a mirage.
Yes, I know that even the wildest man
Can be tamed by a woman. Faced by her
This lioness, the cruellest man
Submits, and when a baby appears,
Cuddles that infant tenderly,
Allows it to finger his prickly beard
And sings it a tentative lullaby.
A farmer's gaze on his golden grain
Is warm, but a father's is twice as warm
When he watches his children and notes how they've grown.
What do I care if my father reforms
If his new children steal my birthright
And I'm forced to carry in my arms
A lioness who will tear me to bits?

Batin   Sir, discreet men, men of good sense,
When they find themselves subjected
To ills that can't be remedied,
Employ their patience
And they feign happiness and trust
So none will think them envious.

Federico	How can I face a step-mother?
Batin	You had plenty of step-mothers when your father Was running wild. Now all that's done You've only got to put up with one.
Federico	What are those cries?
Batin	They're from the ford.
Federico	The cries of women!
Batin	Come back.
Federico	You're afraid. Coward, we're bound to assist a stranger.
Batin	Courage doesn't mean looking for danger, Ricardo! Febo!

[*Enter* RICARDO *and* FEBO]

Ricardo	We are here! Where's Federico?
Febo	I can't see — Does he want the horses?
Batin	A lady yelled And off he charged misguidedly If courageously. My duty's clear — I'll have to follow him.

[*Exit* BATIN]

Febo	Wait for me.
Ricardo	It's some practical joke, for heaven's sake.
Febo	But I can hear, from the riverside An awful kerfuffle.
Ricardo	Let it be. Federico's collecting his father's bride But you'd think he'd been sent to catch a snake.
Febo	That's because he's dissatisfied.

[*Enter* FEDERICO *carrying* CASANDRA *in his arms*]

Federico	I set you down here Softly and safely.
Casandra	Thank you, my knight, You carried me kindly.

Federico	I thank the stars Which led to the fairest Inhabitant Of this far forest.
Casandra	Who are these people?
Federico	My father's servants. All of them, like me, At your service.

[*Enter* BATIN *with* LUCRECIA, *a servant, in his arms*]

Batin	Weighty wench, would you care to alight?
Lucrecia	Where are you taking me, noble knight?
Batin	Not much further. Over this sand Which is treacherous and onto dry land. I think it's the river's idea of a joke To overturn your coach and soak Beautiful nymphs. That river cursed – He'd have ravished you, but I got there first.
Federico	Lady, I know you're nobly born By your appearance and air. I would like to address you properly. Pray, tell me who you are?
Casandra	Sir, there's no call for concealment. I tell you: I am Casandra, The Duchess of Ferrara. My father's the Duke of Mantua.
Federico	But does the Duchess travel With no champion by her side?
Casandra	By Carlos, the Marquis Gonzaga I am accompanied. But I asked him to leave me while my coach took A little track beside the river So I could bathe and rest awhile Till the fierce noon was over. As the coach struggled up the bank Through the thick trees and thicker shadows, The waters rose. Our luck sank. The wheels stopped, stuck in the shallows. I know that you are generous – I cried out, and you came. I know that you are brave as well.

Now please, tell me your name.
I'm deeply in you debt,
But it's not only I.
Carlos and my father
Will thank you by and by.

Federico   After you've given your hand to me
I'll tell you my identity.

Casandra   On your knees? It is not right. It
Goes too far – I can't permit it.

Federico   Madam, it's right and dutifully done.
I must inform you – I am your new son.

Casandra   What a fool I am
Not to recognise you
By your bravery –
Let me embrace you.

Federico   Your hand is enough.

Casandra   It is not right.
Count Federico,
Let my arms pay my debt.
You will allow . . .

Federico   I'll answer with my heart.

[FEDERICO *and* CASANDRA *talk, aside*]

Batin   Since we struck lucky and rescued the lady
Who was the reason for our trip.
All I'm in doubt about,
Have to find out about,
Is, should I call you "Your Ladyship"?

Lucrecia   I'm just a serving maid, only a waiting maid.

Batin   What does it call for, this job you've got?

Lucrecia   I dress her Highness.
I undress her Highness.

Batin   Then you're a chambermaid!

Lucrecia   Certainly not.

Batin   You stay outside
And you dress her inside?
You're a not-quite chambermaid.
What's your name?

Lucrecia	Lucrecia.
Batin	You wouldn't be a Borgia?
Lucrecia	Don't think so.
Batin	The one from Rome?
Lucrecia	Of course not. Mantua is my home.
Batin	You've not heard of Lucretia? You're lucky, you've escaped a Tedious moral story. Tarquin came and raped her. What would you do if you and Tarquin met?
Lucrecia	Sir, I'd like to meet your wife.
Batin	Why'd you want to do that?
Lucrecia	She'd teach me how to Handle you, you rat.
Batin	I'm extremely hurt. Do you know my name?
Lucrecia	How would I know?
Batin	Can it be that the fame Of Batin has not reached as far As the sunny slums Of Mantua?
Lucrecia	What are you famous for? What could that possibly be? The world's most perfect fool Or her greatest nonentity?
Batin	Oh, God, I hope not. I'm sorry. I just tried Too hard to be witty. I'm not self-satisfied. I'm really very humble And quiet as a rule. Perhaps my only wisdom Is knowing I'm a fool. When I first saw Lucrecia I trembled for her touch. I gave her all my nonsense – She gave back twice as much.

Casandra

I still cannot express
My joy at having met you.
They were inadequate,
The things I'd heard about you.
The way you speak and move
Are so harmonious.
My lord, my son, they prove,
With what you did for us,
The qualities which animate the whole
Of your noble, individual soul.

What luck I turned aside
From the road and went
To meet you by mistake
In a lucky accident.
As sailors out at sea
Caught in a deadly storm
Survive courageously
To see the lovely dawn
My coach was the vessel, tempest-torn.
I was the helmsman, you were my dawn.

From this day, Federico,
Pray do me the honour
Of granting me a sacred name
By calling me your mother.
I am so pleased with you,
Such a kind and gentle one.
Glad to be Duchess of Ferrara,
I'm even happier that you're my son.

Federico

Lady, I'm overawed by your beauty's light
And, further, bewildered by the honour you pay me.
Today the Duke, my lord, has split my being
Into two parts. He was my body's author
But now a second birth has given me
My soul, for the first time, my soul is mine.
Two births, my lady, but the birth you give me
Is the more glorious, so I wish today
To be born in spirit, to be born of you.
It is God, I know, who infuses the soul,
But till I saw you, I never felt
How much soul I had. You have made me new.
For I was alive, but I had no soul.
From this you can argue, since I wish you to bear me,
I am that firstborn son the Duke expects from you.

I'm a grown man, and I long to be born.
Well, the sun's six thousand years old, but he's born every
dawn.

[*Enter* CARLOS, *the Marquis of Gonzaga and* RUTILIO]

Rutilio   My lord, I left them here.

Carlos   There would have been a tragedy
                  If the knight of whom you speak
                  Hadn't arrived to rescue her.

Rutilio   She sat down and dismissed me, so
                  Her feet could both enjoy a bath
                  And beat the water into froth
                  And feel the pearly bubbles flow.
                  That's why I wasn't near the place
                  When the trouble started and
                  The Duchess was carried to dry land
                  In that gentleman's embrace.
                  When they were safe, and not before,
                  I ran to fetch you. Ran like mad.

Carlos   Yes. There's the coach, stuck in the mud
                  Between the river and the shore.

Rutilio   She was past the willows and out of sight.
                  There she is with the servants of the knight.

Casandra   Here come my friends

Carlos   My lady!

Casandra   Carlos!

Carlos   The Lord be praised that you're all right

Casandra   Now that you've thanked him, thank this knight.
                  His arms rescued me compassionately.

Carlos   Count, what a trick Heaven has played
                  To make you the one who comes to the aid
                  Of your mother — to name her rightfully.

Federico   I wish that I were Zeus
                  So that I could escape
                  Out of my body now
                  Into an eagle's shape.
                  With my great golden claws
                  I'd clutch her to my breast.
                  Though the sun singed my wings

I would not pause to rest
But carry her through
The dangerous sky
To the arms of the Duke
And her destiny.

Carlos   These events, sir,
Were arranged by Fate
So Casandra's debt to you
Should be great.
Your mutual goodwill
Shall grow like a child
And all Italy's feuds
Shall be reconciled.

[*They continue talking*]

Casandra   While the two of them are talking
Tell me, Lucrecia, what you're thinking
About Federico.

Lucrecia   With your permission
May I give you my opinion?

Casandra   I think I know what you're going to say.
But say on —

Lucrecia   — I think, in a way . . .

Casandra   Well?

Lucrecia   I think that you'd have fared
Better if Fate had given you the son.

Casandra   Exactly so, Lucrecia, and Fate
Has blundered, but what's done is done.
If I returned, on some pretext or other
Home to Mantua suddenly,
I'm sure I'd be killed by my father.
Throughout the length of Italy
My folly would be infamous.
Federico can't marry me,
So turning back now would be senseless.
To travel hopelessly is better than to arrive.
So I'll keep travelling, hopelessly,
Towards Ferrara and it's Duke,
That habitual sensualist
Of whose outrages as a rake
I have obtained a detailed list.

Carlos	Friends, take your horses. We must ride Out of this dangerous Countryside. Rutilio – Ride ahead and tell The anxious Duke That all is well Or he'll only hear Of our disaster. Good news is slow, Bad news runs faster. Come with me, madam. Oh, somebody might Get a horse for the Count.
Febo	That one's all right.
Casandra	My coach is comfortable. Your excellency Would be best advised To travel with me.
Federico	I will travel with you Any way. Command me, lady, And I obey.

[CARLOS *leads* CASANDRA *off by the hand,* FEDERICO *and* BATIN *remain*]

Batin	She's the kindest Duchess I've ever seen.
Federico	Then you appove of her, Batin?
Batin	[*Sings*] Oh she's the white lily Who stands on a lawn And her four snowy tongues Sing this song to the dawn: "Send diamond dew-drops, I want them to wear And I'll give you gold-dust, Pretty gold-dust for your hair." [*Speaks*] I've not seen such beauty since I was small. By God, sir, if it wasn't so late – (They're mounting now – don't make her wait,) I'd say –

Federico	— Better say nothing at all. You looked into my eyes and saw my soul. So you say what you know I want you to say.
Batin	She'd suit you better, obviously. This rosebud and orange-blossom bouquet, This sweetness, this amber and gold confection, This Venus, this Helen, this perfection. How harsh the laws of this world can be!
Federico	Batin, we mustn't make them suspicious. I think I must be the first step-child To find his step-mother delicious.
Batin	Sir, just be patient for a while. When she's scolded you once or twice, young man, She'll seem ugly as an orang-utan

[*Exeunt*]

Scene Three

[*The Palace of the* DUKE *of Ferrara*]

[*Enter the* DUKE *of Ferrara and* AURORA, *his niece*]

Duke	Federico will meet her on the way.
Aurora	Of course, for they ride Along the same road.
Duke	I think that Federico may Be travelling slowly, angrily, For he expected to be my heir And all his expectations were Based upon promises by me. He knows I love him. My dear son. Marriage? I didn't intend to do it But my subjects urged me to it, Convincing me it must be done. They love him, Aurora, as they love me, But, if my son were to succeed Claimants would rise on every side Challenging his legitimacy. Long-lost kinsmen would stake their claims, A family quarrel would catch fire And then it wouldn't be long before Half of Ferrara perished in flames.

Civil War – it's the ordinary people who
Suffer most terribly. So I found
It necessary to change my mind
When they counselled marriage. What else could I do?

Aurora   Sir, you are not to blame.
It was Fortune's fault.
But we should try to take
The sting from Federico's plight.
He's disappointed
To lose the succession.
I'd like to offer
A bold suggestion.
I am the daughter of the brother you lost
When, like the premature almond tree
Which proffers its blossoms to the frost –
He was twenty-five – he was taken from me.
And then my mother died, like some frail flower.
You fondly brought me up, so I can say:
In the blind labyrinth of my dark hour
You were the gold thread, leading to the day.
So Federico was brought up with me
·And gradually there grew
An ever-honest intimacy –
We shared one life between the two.
One law, one love, one will, one faith.
Now marriage would make our love life-long.
He's mine and I am his and even Death
Dare not destroy a bond so sweet and strong.
My wealth has thrived so prettily,
No dowry is finer
In all the land of Italy.
(There may be richer brides in China).
Marry me to him. I'll take care
That he'll not pine away.
Casandra may give you an heir –
My love will save the day.

Duke   Come to my heart, Aurora,
For, in my brooding night,
You are the dawn from heaven
Bringing the kindly light.
My malady is passing
And by your light I see
As in the clearest mirror –
You bring my remedy.

You save my state and honour.
I promise him to you
If the way in which you win him
Is, like your own love, true.
And since your loving feelings
Are mutual, as you say,
I give my word that we shall have
Two weddings on one day.
When the Count arrives – just wait and see –
Ferrara shall explode with celebrations.

Aurora   I am your daughter and your slave.

[*Enter* BATIN]

Batin   Your Highness, divide your congratulations
Between me and the wind, for, honoured master,
I don't know which of us two came first
In the race to get here. First I was faster,
Then the wind, then me, then we both burst.
The fact that the Duchess is unhurt'll
Astonish you when you know of her plight.
The flood caught her coach, the coach turned turtle,
But everything turned out all right
For up rode the Count, that gallant young man,
Galloping hell for leather,
To disprove that stepsons and stepmothers can
Never get on together.
They speak so harmoniously that one
Would think them a mother and her son.

Duke   Batin, this friendship between the two
Is the best news you bring.
Indeed for the Count to be carefree at all
Is a new and unusual thing.
God grant that their love may grow.
He saved her, did he?

Batin   Even so.
Fortune smiles upon those two.

Aurora   I also require some news from you.

Batin   Aurora, whose name, irresistibly
Would fire the prosiest idiot
To rosy-fingered simile –

Aurora   Is she beautiful or is she not?

Batin	You know already by hearsay.
	Besides, I think that this is more
	A matter for the Duke today.
	That's enough. They're outside the door.

[DUKE *presents* BATIN *with a chain*]

Duke	Batin, you have been my mainstay.

[*Enter, with much splendour,* FEBO, RICARDO, CARLOS, FEDERICO, CASANDRA *and* LUCRECIA]

Federico	Madam, in the orchard
	Stands a glorious pavillion
	With silver silks
	And golden flags
	And banners blue and green.
	For you, her noble Duchess,
	Ferrara is preparing
	The greatest celebration
	Italy has seen.
Casandra	But now there's a strange silence . . .
	A disappointing greeting.
Ricardo	Silence for the Duke of Ferrara!
Febo	And blessings on this meeting!
Duke	God keep you fair Casandra.
	To you I freely offer
	The brave state of Ferrara.
	Accept, and do us honour.
Casandra	Great lord, I am your humble slave,
	That's what I've come to be.
	And I know that title does
	Honour to all my family,
	Honour to my father
	And honour to Mantua, too.
	So I have gladly travelled here
	To be a bride for you.
Duke	Carlos, let's embrace.
	Let me thank you for this prize.
Carlos	I am rewarded if I can play
	Some part in the coming ceremonies.
Aurora	Casandra. I'm Aurora.

Casandra	Among all new gifts I find One brighter than the others – You are to be my friend.
Aurora	Casandra, I will serve you, Love you with all I am. Ferrara is most fortunate That you make it your home.
Casandra	My new life begins so auspiciously I'm sure I shall spend it most happily.
Duke	Be seated, so that lovingly My kin and my household May welcome you respectfully.
Casandra	I do as I am told, Sir and sit at your command.

[*The* DUKE, CASANDRA, CARLOS *and* AURORA *sit under a canopy*]

	May not the Count sit with us too?
Duke	No, he must kiss your hand.
Casandra	Forgive me, I cannot allow Such subservience. –
Federico	Do not insult my love for you Or my obedience.
Casandra	I don't want you to obey.
Federico	I'm trembling.
Casandra	Stop.
Federico	Don't stop me now. I kiss your hand three times, lady. One of the kisses is for you To pledge I'll be yours as long as I live, An example to all Ferrara. The second kiss for the Duke's sake I give, My lord, whom I most humbly honour, The third kiss – that is for your sake. First I fulfilled my duty to you. Next I obeyed the command of the Duke. Now I pay homage because I want to. Unprompted, I swear my constancy And my heartfelt loyalty. Let my arms form a chain For your dutiful neck.

Duke	Federico is courteous.
Carlos	So is the Duke. Aurora, I've been told so much about you That, meeting you, I'm both happy and nervous. I have never seen such beauty before. All I can hope is to be at your service.
Aurora	Marquis, I'll treasure this compliment For you're famous throughout all Italy For lion-like courage on the battlefield Rather than eloquent courtesy. You're both a soldier and a courtier, hence You pay courageous compliments.
Carlos	I take those words as my cue to swear That from now on I am your knight And your champion in Ferrara. With a high heart I will fight A thousand knights if they should dare Maintain their ladies are as fair.
Duke	Now I expect you'd like to rest. Prolonging welcome ceremonies Would show that lack of consideration Which, my married friends have warned me, is The worst of vices. Love shall not say I was a man who threw good luck away.

[*Exit all except* FEDERICO *and* BATIN]

Federico	Oh my poor mind! What stupid thoughts.
Batin	What's the matter? Out of sorts?
Federico	They say life's a dream And that's well said For not only when We're asleep in bed. But when we're awake Our imaginings Can be more terrible Than the things Which into the head Of a sick man come When he burns in fever's Delirium.

Batin   Too true, that often happens to me.
                        I'll be hanging about with a group of men,
                        Thinking of nothing much, and then
                        An urge comes over me suddenly
                        To bash one of my fiends on the nut
                        Or give another a vampire bite!
                        I may be perfectly happy, but,
                        If I'm up a tower, I feel I might
                        Dive and get splattered all about.
                        When I'm in a church, and with great aplomb
                        The priest gives a sermon, I want to shout:
                        "I've read the book you nicked that from!"
                        I want to giggle whenever I go
                        To funerals. When two tough and slick
                        Sailors play dice – it's the final throw –
                        I want to crown them with the candlestick.
                        When great singers start singing I want to sing too.
                        And when I see a lady with a hair-do
                        Like the Tower of Pisa in stormy weather
                        I want to pull out the ribbons that hold it together,
                        And it's such a strong feeling, I blush till I bleed,
                        As if I'd performed the mischievous deed.

Federico   Jesus! God help me! A crowd of insane
                        Daydreams are storming the streets of my brain!
                        How could I think such a thing,
                        Imagine such a thing,
                        Say such a thing,
                        Or expect such a thing?
                        No more! No more of this mad raving.

Batin   Have I shocked you with my wildness?

Federico   No – for you've never done such things.
                        You cannot be blamed for fancies
                        Which are no more than vapourings.

Batin   Are you hiding some deep, troubled thoughts from me?

Federico   If I hide my thoughts, I hide nothing, truly,
                        For I think of what's not, and what must not be.

Batin   Suppose I tell you what you're thinking –
                        Will you deny it?

Federico   Before you can guess
                        The sky will be full of daisies, twinkling
                        And dewy stars will grow among the grass.

Batin	I'll guess. You inform me if I lie. Federico, you don't know what to do Since your stepmother caught your eye.
Federico	Don't say it, Batin, for it's true. But I can't help this error, for A man's thoughts fly at liberty.
Batin	They fly so far, they're a mirror for Our spirit's immortality.
Federico	Can we say the Duke's lucky?
Batin	I think we can.
Federico	Despite the whole thing's impossibility I am becoming jealous of the man.
Batin	Well, that is a reasonable jealousy. Casandra is better suited to you.
Federico	And I may well die of this new, Impossible love. Isn't that true?

[*Exeunt*]

[*End of Act One*]

Act 2

[*The* DUKE's *palace*]

[LUCRECIA *is brushing* CASANDRA's *hair*]

Casandra [*Sings*]
In my swansdown bed
I awake at dawn
And I'm face to face
With a great lord's scorn.
If I slept on straw
With some peasant lad
His good morning kisses
They would make me glad.
Yes, I'd rather be
A poor country girl.

And I wish to God
That each night I lay
With a loving ploughman
Who worked all day.
When the moonlight falls
On the poor and rich
And they're at their loving
Who knows which is which
But I'd rather be
A poor country girl.

Oh the sun shines through
Crystal window panes
On a lonely lady
In golden chains.
Oh the sun shines down
On an old hay-cart
Where two naked bodies
Share a single heart
And I'd rather be
A poor country girl.

For the country girl
Is a cherished bride
And she rises happy
From her husband's side
And she sees her face

In a spring nearby
And she sings and washes
And she does not cry
And I'd rather be
That poor country girl.

[*Speaks*]
Than the wife of any faithless man –
Even the Duke of Ferrara!

He spent just one night in my bed.
Months have passed since I realised
He wanted nothing more from me.

I can tell you, Lucrecia, at least.
But why should I complain? I knew
About his old wild way of life.
The devil doesn't take a halo
Just because he takes a wife.
A man may come home with the dawn
And live just as he likes
Subject to no married rules –
These are a man's rights.
But to treat a lady contemptuously
When he's just become her master –
Either he's the fool of fools
Or he's hungry for disaster.
The Duke must be one of those men
Who thinks a wife is meant
To be one of his household goods,
Kept as an ornament.
A little painting on the wall,
A desk, a chair, a bed.
It's wrong. If she is treated well
No wife goes to the bad.
When a woman wants to be a wife
Naturally she gets wed.
She wants to be a wife, and not
A desk, a chair, a bed.
But if her husband becomes rude,
Showing her no gratitude,
That wife's thoughts will begin to stray
And there'll be trouble one fine day.

Lucrecia   Casandra, I'm sorry and amazed
At the way he serves you.
Who would have thought the married Duke

Would prove to be so scurvy?
If he won't make love to you
He might at least take care
To act politely, so your hurt
Is easier to bear.
With an admirer who's luke-warm
You can rouse his jealousy
And make him anxious by your scorn
Or flirting while he's standing by
Or praising some man to the sky –
All these things make men hot.
We play such tricks on wooers,
But on husbands, better not.
Have you written to Mantua
To tell this to your father?

Casandra   No, my eyes are the only ones
Who know how I fare in Ferrara.

Lucrecia   It would have been more natural
And have shown more common sense
If you had been married
To Federico, since
That way the duke's estate could go
To his first grandson.
Federico's melancholy fit
Is not a groundless one.

Casandra   Don't you think he's envious,
Lucrecia, and that's caused by me?
But I'll not give him brothers
And so the Count may be
Sure that I'll do him no injury.
This marriage damages both him and me.

[*Enter the* DUKE, FEDERICO *and* BATIN]

Duke   Count, had I imagined that
My marriage would make you unhappy
I'd have died sooner than envisage it.

Federico   Sir, it would be absurd of me
To be grieved by your marriage, nor do I doubt
You love me because you happen to marry.
Your keen mind must have worked this out –
Were I unhappy for that cause
I'd hide my grief. There is about
My soul a pallor, it shows in my face
But no-one knows the cause.

Duke	The doctors said They could not diagnose your case, But you'd recover when you've wed.
Federico	Sir, that might cure a maiden's pain. I'm not so easily comforted.
Casandra	There's blank rudeness and rare disdain! The Duke has scarcely glanced at me.
Lucrecia	If he did not see you that'd explain His action.
Casandra	Pretending not to see? Let's leave, Lucrecia; If I'm not mistaken One day he will pay for this insult to me.

[*Exit* CASANDRA *and* LUCRECIA]

Duke	Your most suitable bride is at this court, No foreigner, one that you hold dear.
Federico	Aurora?
Duke	You have snatched the thought Out of mind, as if you read it clear, Considered it, liked it, learned it by heart. Marry – your injuries will disappear.
Federico	Sir, you can't see what's in my heart. Why should you think that I'm depressed Because I'm wronged? Sir, for my part You know I never have expressed Even the slightest disapproval Of your marriage, it seemed for the best.
Duke	I believe you and always have done. Oh, now I regret I got married at all For you prove such an obedient son.
Federico	Sir, don't suspect that I'm resentful. How could I criticise something so right? I would like to repay your love in full. First I'll find out if my cousin might Be willing – if so, obediently. And as you wish, our loves shall unite.
Duke	She told me. She'll marry you willingly.
Federico	But times have changed. There's something new. Carlos lingers here, for she Emboldens him to stay and woo.

Duke   Federico, what's that to you?

Federico   When a man wants to marry, it seems improper
                    For his bride to be chased by another suitor.
                    Two clerks can't write on the same sheet of paper.

Duke   You're like a man who sees his daughter
                    Smiled at one day when she's a child
                    So thinks it politic to shut her
                    Up in a tower till she's old.
                    Look at yourself in a flawless glass.
                    Your breath is warm, the mirror's cold,
                    And so a cloud obscures your face.
                    But if you keep looking in the mirror,
                    Soon it will clear, and clear it stays.

Federico   Sir, your rebuke is apt and clever.
                    But sir, when the furnace of a forge spits out
                    Brilliant sparks and the smith endeavours
                    To quench the crackling fire's heart,
                    The flames greedily drink down the water
                    And then rise up, seeming twice as hot.
                    And so the husband who ignores a lover
                    Quenches his bride's first amorous flame
                    But that fire may flare up more fiercely than ever.
                    If a woman's on fire for another man
                    I don't want to be water, exciting the blaze,
                    Setting fire to my honour and my good name.

Duke   Count, you're a fool and impertinent.
                    What you say of the lady is quite untrue.
                    Your remarks verge on the indecent.

Federico   Now, wait sir!

Duke   I'll not wait for you.

                    [*Exit the* DUKE]

Batin   Nice work, throwing away
                    The Duke's favour —

Federico   I might as well
                    Throw it away
                    And dive into hell.
                    Batin, my despair
                    Is so great that I
                    Will only escape it
                    When I die.

And if I should die
I'll be born again
One thousand times
So I may attain
One thousand deaths –
But God won't give
Me enough courage
To die or live.
For it's death to me
If I live on.
If I murdered myself
My pain would be gone
So I would murder
Myself in vain.
I must go on living
For I love my pain.

Batin   From all of this count,
You seem to imply
That you can't bear to live
And you don't want to die,
So you're stuck in the middle,
Neither left or right
Like a half-alive, half-dead
Hermaphrodite.
By God, you're so desperate
I must request
The desperate reasons
Which make you distressed.
So give me the truth
Or permission to leave
So that all alone, loyally,
I can grieve.
Give me your hand.

Federico   If I could tell
What my ailment is
It might soon be well.
For an illness which
Can be spoken about
Is an illness which
Can be cast out.
My illness is such
My reason rejects it
And only my five senses

Seem to accept it.
It would help to talk
So I talk, or try,
But the distance between
The earth and the sky
Is less than the distance
Between my heart
And my stumbling tongue.
Batin, depart,
Leave me here alone.
I'm less than the shadow
Of a stone.

[*Enter* CASANDRA *and* AURORA]

Casandra   You cry over that?

Aurora   Why shouldn't I?
Federico hates me –
I've the right to cry.
He says that I love
Carlos. Not true.
But I think I know
What he's trying to do.
He's made up his mind
To sneak away,
For before his father's
Wedding day
I was the very
Light of his eyes.
But now he's expelled me
From paradise.
Aurora could once
Banish the night
And the Count would come seeking
His eyes' delight.
Is there a fountain
Or willow tree
Where the Count has not sworn
His love for me?
Were not these lips
And features of mine
Compared to jasmine
And columbine?
When we were apart
He could barely survive

                        And lived for the moment
                        When I'd arrive
                        Back in his arms
                        Where our hearts had grown
                        So entangled they formed
                        One heart alone.
                        Born with our births
                        Must our great love die
                        Because of a man's
                        Changeability?
                        Ambition committed
                        This deed because
                        He wanted his Dukedom –

Casandra   Yes, I'm the cause.
                        Aurora, I'm sorry,
                        But curb your anxiety,
                        I'll talk him out of
                        His cruel jealousy.

Aurora   Jealousy?

Casandra   Over Carlos, yes.
                        That's what the Duke says.

Aurora   Oh, your highness
                        May be sure Federico's
                        Melancholy
                        Is neither from love
                        Nor jealousy.

                        [*Exit* AURORA]

Casandra   Federico.

Federico   Oh my lady,
                        Give the fair hand of the duchess
                        To your slave.

Casandra   Why do you kneel?
                        Count, please end this show of meekness.
                        I'll call you "Your Excellency".

Federico   That would insult my love and deepen
                        New wounds. I don't intend to rise
                        Without your hand.

Casandra   My arms are open.
                        What's wrong with you? Look in my face.
                        What do you see there? Federico,

You're trembling. Do you realise
How much I love you?

Federico   Yes, my soul guessed,
Ran to my heart and told it.
My heart told my face
Which cannot hide it.

Casandra   Batin, I must talk with the Count
So leave us here alone.

Batin   The Count and Casandra both upset —
God knows what's going on!

[*Exit* BATIN]

Federico   I'm dying like the Phoenix.
Do not fan the flames.
I don't want another life.
Don't want to be born again.

Casandra   Federico, I've considered
The tale told by Aurora
That you've been stung by jealousy
Since I came to Ferrara
Accompanied by the Marquis.
Now she says, because of this,
You do not want to marry her.
Well, I believe you underrate
Your virtues and good sense
Because, perhaps you've given way
To envy and to diffidence.
The Marquis shines? Yes, I concur,
But many ladies would prefer
A courtier's to a soldier's brilliance.
So I believe my marriage
To the Duke's the cause
Of this deep dejection
And misery of yours.
Because, if I should bear his son
All your hopes will be undone —
Federico — a lost cause.

Now since it's I who cause you this
Spiritual agony,
Let me disillusion you —
You will never see
Any brother usurp your throne.

The Duke's a husband for one reason alone –
That's what his subjects want him to be.

The Duke's debaucheries –
I'm trying to be polite,
Have allowed him to be in my arms
For less than one short night,
Although, according to his jeers,
It felt more like a hundred years.
After this very brief respite
He has returned to his old haunts
With renewed lust, of course.
He broke the bridle of my arms
Like a spirited, wild horse
Who shies suddenly and rears
When the drumbeat hurts his ears.
(I try, you see, not to be coarse).
And the horse bolts, scattering round
Trappings of fine embroidery,
Pieces of bridle and the bit,
Spraying like foam and flashing by,
There go the reins, there goes the bridle,
There go the straps, there goes the saddle –
There goes the Duke, having broken free
From the bonds of matrimony,
Let loose on the women of the town,
Scattering fragments of his fame.
Here he leaves his title behind,
There, he scatters his good name,
The honour of his ancestry,
His body's health, his bravery –
Gambled away in this deadly game.
He wastes his time, he wastes himself,
He turns night into day
With his despicable ribaldry.
So please believe me when I say
You will inherit his estate
For Federico, I shall write
To my fierce father, begging him
To come and set me free
From this palace prison
Unless death comes first to me
And ends all my misery.

Federico   You started by scolding me
                      But your speech

Has ended in tears
Which would stamp a seal
Of sorrow on granite.
What are you doing?
I can see I'm judged
As the son of the man
Who's your husband, who wrongs you.
But I'll make this clear:
When he acts unjustly
I'm no son of his.
Madam, I'm shocked
You imagine my grief
Springs from such base motives.
Does Federico
Need a state to rule
To be who he is,
To be Federico?
If I married my cousin
Would I not have
All her estates?
If I went to war
With a neighbouring prince,
Wouldn't I keep
Every acre I plundered?
Sure I am sad,
But it's not for myself,
Not for self-interest.
I say more than I should.
But, Madam, please know,
My story's the saddest
Since Eros first set
Arrow to bowstring.
Death comes relentlessly.
My life flickers out
Like a candle flame,
Little by little,
And I beg death
Not to let it burn down
But to blow it out now
And cover my years
With merciful night.

Casandra   Federico, hold back your tears.
God did not give to men
The gift of weeping, but courage.

Nature entitled woman
To weep when they like because
Though they are courageous
They're denied the right to act.
But there is just one time
Men are allowed to weep –
If their honour's lost they may weep
While they wipe out the affront.
A curse upon Aurora
For arousing jealousy.
She's reduced a gallant man,
Who's so worthy of being loved
To such a state of misery.

Federico   You are wrong. It's not Aurora.

Casandra   Who is it?

Federico   The sun herself.
There are many Auroras
But there is only one sun.

Casandra   Not Aurora?

Federico   My thoughts fly higher.

Casandra   Could a woman see you and talk with you
And hear you tell of your love
And yet ungratefully tell you
She does not return your love?
I say it's impossible.

Federico   If you knew what impossible meant
You'd say it's impossible I'm a man
Or I'd have died of pain.
You'd say that I'm still living
Is some kind of miracle.
Who can equal my presumption?
Phaeton perhaps, who stole
The chariot of the sun?
Unlucky Icarus who
Stuck together with wax
A fragile frame of feathers
Which, scattered on the breeze
Made the ocean look up and think
A flock of birds was passing
Till they fluttered down to fall
All over her salty surface?

Bellerophon riding upon
Mighty-winged Pegasus,
Who looked down and saw the world
Like a singing circle of the stars?
Sinon, the Greek who led
That horse pregnant with soldiers
In through the yawning gates of Troy,
That horse which gave birth
To the flames of death?
Jason, the first to attempt
To cross the oceans, who bore
Like a yoke across his shoulders
The masts and sails of Argos?
Tell me which one of these
Could equal my presumption?

Casandra   Tell me Count, are you in love
With a statue of bronze, a nymph
Or a goddess of alabaster?
The souls of woman are not
Like flies suspended in amber
Or mammoths in glaciers.
They are clothed in the lightest gauze
Which covers all human thoughts.
Love never called out to a heart
Without the soul replying:
"I am here, but enter softly."
Tell your love, whoever she is.
It's not a coincidence that the Greeks
Sometimes show Venus in the arms
Of a satyr or faun. The moon is high,
But look, she walked down her silvery stairs
A thousand times for Endymion's sake.
Federico, take my advice,
The best-guarded fortress
Has gates made of wax.
Speak from your soul,
Don't die of silence.

Federico   You know how they catch the Indian pelican.

[*Sings*]
The hunter lights a fire
All round the nest
Of the Indian pelican.

The pelican flies down
To save its young
And its wings beat furiously.

Those wingbeats fan the flames
The flames grow tall
Both the wings are burned away.

Defenceless on the ground
The bird is caught
Never knowing it would be

Alive if it had flown
And fled away
That sad Indian pelican.

My thoughts, which are the young
Of my soul's love
Hidden in their silent nest.

My thoughts are catching fire,
Love beats its wings
And the flames are fanned by them.

And now my love's on fire,
The flames grow tall
And my wings are burned away.

You smile and I'm on fire.
You laugh. I'm lost.
You inspire me, and I gaze.

First you encourage me,
I cannot move.
Set me free, I chain myself.

You raise me to the sky
I'm still on earth.
Show the way, but I'm ashamed.

The land I walk across
Is dangerous
Death is all that I can see.

I think my only course
Is suffering
And dying soon and silently.

[*Exit* FEDERICO]

Casandra   [*Sings*]
Humanity received a thousand gifts

On the Sixth Day of Creation
But of the thousand gifts the worst by far —
The power of imagination.

Imagination turns our peace to war
And it changes ice to fire
Imagination taunts our thirsty minds
With mirages of our desire.

And now my heart is stumbling in the dark
And it needs illumination.
Illusions crowd around instead of light
All thanks to my imagination.

[*Speaks*]

His shadowy hinting,
His obvious confusions.
He did no explaining,
I'm left with guesses.
He's destroyed my calm
Like a mighty wind
For the greatest storms
Are set loose in the mind.
When I feel I have won
Federico's affection
I am told by my reason
It's out of the question.
When I face my fate
As an unhappy bride
Then I hide my face
For I have to cry.
But nothing I find
Is so impossible
That the eye of the mind
Can't render it visible.

I'm invaded and mobbed
By feelings and facts.
My husband's a devil.
Must I go mad?
O sometimes my doom
Seems so easy to change
That I feel that the time
Is ripe for revenge.
But that vengeance is so
Atrocious a deed

That my joy casts a shadow
Shaped like a sword.

The Count's kind and good
But to give way to passion
Would prove I were mad
Despite the temptation.
Heaven defend me!
If wishing is sinful
There cannot be any
Men who are honourable.
But so far my honour's
Committed no error
It just glanced at sin like
A face in a mirror.
To yield in one's heart
Is a sin in God's eyes
But honour's not hurt
For it sees otherwise.
God knows our thoughts, and weighs up every one,
But honour only judges by what's done.

[*Enter* AURORA]

Aurora   You and the Count have been talking
A long time, what does he say?

Casandra   He says he returns your love
That is his reply.
All he asks of you, Aurora,
Is – cause him no jealousy.

[*Exit* CASANDRA]

Aurora   Well, that's luke-warm comfort
For my anxiety!
Once he loved my every thought.
Now he's transformed by frustration
At the way Casandra's brought
An end to his hopes of succession.
Love, you are mighty –
You control
My life, my honour,
Even my soul.
Love, you are feeble.
He loved me, and yet
Now his love's crushed
By Casandra's threat.

Since he's pretended
To be jealous
And jealousy
Makes a cool lover zealous
I'll try to rouse his jealousy
By flirting with Carlos publicly.

[*Enter* RUTILIO *and* CARLOS]

Rutilio   You've got no hope with her.

Carlos   I find
New hope whenever I say her name.
Aurora! She's coming.

Rutilio   What a shame
That you're out, as usual, of your mind.

Carlos   Aurora, recall that shining day
Whan I first wondered at your face
And, in that moment, gave my heart away?
You shine, and end my painful night,
The colours of the world return,
The dawn breaks from your lips of light.
But though I state my ardour, honestly,
And though I passionately make my case,
My wooing only makes you tire of me.
Seeing you was bad luck, although
I never saw such a light before.
You turn my day to night, and I must go.
I'll travel to some foreign land.
New love, perhaps, in a new place.
Give me your leave. Give me your hand.

Aurora   If you give up so easily
You'll never die of sorrow.
Well, that's a comfort, but not courtesy.
Carlos, why faint at the first rebuff?
Love's favours should not be granted
Until love has grown strong enough.
Your love's a little one, and so
Your pain's a little one as well.
Well, I command you not to go.

Carlos   Madam, you speak severely
But it will give me joy
To stay ten times the ten years
The Greeks laid siege to Troy.

No, longer, for like Tantalus,
Your love may keep me fasting
Between your kindness and disdain
For ages everlasting.
I pray and hope my love for you
May some day meet success.

Aurora   [*Aside*]
Suffering's better than nothing
When we can't have happiness.

[*Enter* DUKE, FEDERICO *and* BATIN]

Duke   I must leave for Rome.
The Pope has summoned me.

Federico   What's the reason he gives?

Duke   I've no time to reply.
I have to go now.

Federico   If you don't want to tell me
Of course I won't ask.

Duke   When did I ever
Have secrets from you?
I can only tell you
What I suspect.
The wars he's waging
In Italy call for
A much larger army.
I think he's intending
To make me his general,
And if that's the case
He'll expect me to help
Pay the army as well.

Federico   You were right to conceal
The matter in hand
If you wanted to ride off
Without a companion.
But I'm coming with you
For you'll never find
A loyaller soldier
To ride at your side.

Duke   I cannot allow it,
It wouldn't be right
For both of us, Count,

To abandon the state.
Stay and govern it, please,
No-one else will do.
It is right,
I desire it,
That must be enough.

Federico   My lord, I don't want
To offend you at all
But if I remain
What will Italy say?

Duke   Let Italy say:
This is statesmanship.
Or let Italy say:
The Duke cannot stand
His own son's company.

Federico   This is a great test
Of my obedience.

[*Exit* DUKE]

Batin   While you consulted with the Duke
What did Aurora do, sir?
She stared in the eyes of Carlos,
Completely ignoring you, sir.

Federico   Carlos?

Batin   Yes sir,
Stared into his eyes.

Federico   Who cares?

Aurora   This ribbon
Shows where my favour lies.

Carlos   Let it be a chain around my neck,
A fetter to my wrist.
Ask me to wear it, I'll keep it on
As long as I exist.

Aurora   [*Aside*]
This is a just revenge for love,
Though love's what I'd prefer.

[*Aloud*]
Please do me the honour
Of wearing my ribbon, sir.

Batin	Nature's exceedingly subtle.

Batin Nature's exceedingly subtle.
When she made women false –
By that I mean most women,
There are exceptions of course –
For if women weren't grievous deceivers
They'd be totally worshipped by men,
They'd be prayed to and given cathedrals
And what would poor God do then?
Do you see the ribbon?

Federico   What ribbon?

Batin What ribbon? That ribbon! Oh sir,
I remember you called her dawn goddess,
Your heart belonged only to her.
You thought that the planets span round her
And stars perched and sang on her lips.
Has this shooting star plunged in the ocean?
Or is she in total eclipse?
I remember a time when that ribbon
Would have roused a storm like that which tossed
Poor Paris when he'd made his judgement
And told Juno and Pallas "You've lost".

Federico I remember that time, but it's over.

Aurora Shall we walk beside the lake?

[*Exit* AURORA, CARLOS *and* RUTILIO]

Batin He asks for her hand, she gives it,
    Off they go like duck and drake.

Federico Look, they're both young and good friends too.
Why shouldn't they? It's a fine day.

Batin It's a fine day? Are you crazy?

Federico Well, what would you like me to say?

Batin [*Sings*]
If one male swan
Sees a second male swan
Near his female swan
And she looks a bit fond,
The first male swan
Tells the female swan:
Pack up your eggs,
We'll find a new pond.

If a barnyard cock
Finds another fine cock
With his favourite hens
And he's turning their heads.
Why the barnyard cock
Grabs the other cock's comb,
Digs in his beak
And tears him to shreds.

And here are you
And the Marquis is here
And Aurora's here
And they're cooing away.
And here you stand
Like a parakeet,
All you can say
Is: It's a fine day!

Federico If a woman tries to make you jealous
By flirting with another man –
Punish him by letting him have her.

Batin Could you write down this subtle plan?
Or perhaps it's in some courtship manual
Which vagabonds and tinkers sell?
No there's more to it, for love's thought
Is a bucket lowered down a well.
If you want a fresh bucket of water,
Empty the water that's stale.
But why lower the bucket again
When sweet water brims in the pail?
You empty out Aurora
To fill up with – somebody . . .

Federico Batin, if you love me, spare me
Your homespun philosophy.
My soul speaks a strange language
Even I don't comprehend.
The Duke? Has the Duke left yet?
Go and find out, my friend.

Batin You think I'm a fool, but that doesn't matter.
You'd think I was wise if I were to flatter.

[*Exit* BATIN]

Federico Vision of the impossible, please say
What do you want? What do you urge me to?

Why casually throw my life away
And fly where nobody can follow you?
End your wild wanderings near and far
Should you continue, both of us will die.
Vision, give me some peace and do not mar
Golden adventures with black tragedy.
No vision ever came to anything
Or grew, unless seen clear and bright.
With hope, we can bear anything.
All things are visible in love's great light.
Vision, my eyes created you to be
Forever an impossibility.

[*Enter* CASANDRA]

Casandra   Step softly, love, picking your way between
Injuries, revenge and indecisions
And these dishonourable hopes of mine.
On impossible foundations
You can't build a house of happiness.
Because of the wrongs done by the Duke
My soul leans towards wickedness,
I'm like a madwoman, trying to take
Revenge and pleasure at the same time
By committing the greatest possible crime.
The noble, prudent Count will be
The key to open revenge's gates
But there must be total secrecy
Because the felony's so great.
I can read Federico's mind,
It trembles in the balance.
It is most easy to understand
A man who speaks through silence.
My soul loves his uneasiness.
Since the Duke gives me reason
There is a voice inside me says:
Such love can be no treason.

And should I surrender hopelessly
To such a fine man, I believe
The last woman to fall would not be me
Nor the last one to deceive.
History tells us of many daughters
Who fell in love with fathers.
My position's not inhuman –
Sisters have loved their brothers.

Yet precedents for evil
Cannot grant me permission.
To quote an old example
Can't justify my passion.
Enough of this —
The Count is here.
My mind's made up.
Why should I fear?

Federico   Here she comes, the unsheathed sword
Which dooms me. Stars, may we be spared!

Casandra   Federico, are you in distress?

Federico   There seems no end to my sadness.

Casandra   Ill-health causes most melancholy.

Federico   Some strange thoughts have been troubling me.

Casandra   What kind of thoughts, Count? May I learn?

Federico   Madam, they're solely my concern.

Casandra   If there's something I can do,
What is it? Let me hear.

Federico   I would put all my trust in you
But I'm held back by fear.

Casandra   You told me love had you in its spell.

Federico   It causes my pain and my joy as well.

Casandra   A young man, Antiochus,
Became ill when he fell
Deeply in love with his stepmother.

Federico   If he died of it, he did well.

Casandra   His father sent for doctors
To give his son some ease
But he would not admit to them
That love was his disease.

But then there came a doctor
Far wiser than the rest
Who said; "There is a poison
Inside the young man's breast."

The doctor held the young man's wrist
And to his father said:
"Let all the ladies in this place
Pass by the patient's bed."

And when his stepmother walked by
His pulse was twice as quick
So that the doctor knew at once
Why that young man was sick.

Federico   What an igenious idea!

Casandra   Admirable, too.

Federico   Was he cured?

Casandra   Do not deny
I've seen the same in you.

Federico   Did it make you angry, though?

Casandra   Did it make me angry? No.

Federico   Do you pity my distress?

Casandra   Do I feel sorry for you? Yes.

Federico   Well, madam, now I've lost my fear of God
And lost my fear of my own father, too,
I'm in the deepest dungeon of despair
To see my love's impossibility.
I'll try to sum things up. I find myself
Without myself, without God, without you.
Without myself, for I am not with you.
Without God, for I burn to be with you.
Without you, for I cannot make you mine.
If you don't understand, let me explain
So you may see how you've aroused my soul.
They say annihilation's the worst thing,
To be dead nothing in the endless dark.
Madam, I find myself in such a state
Because of you, that to escape this state
I could wish, passionately, not to be.
And so, I walk the paths of hell, since I
Have lost myself, and though I do not wish
Ever again to see myself, I find
That, in the end, madam, I have to look
To see if I'm the same man that I was.
For I am in that state where I don't dare
Even to say that I am who I am.
I'm in a storm, I'm hurled on jagged rocks,
The waves rise over me, death-cold, death-black.
So I've forgotten that this life
I dedicate to you, is owed to God.

But my imprisonment in hell must be
Blamed on us both, for I forgot myself
Because of you, madam, and so I am
Without myself, without God, without you.
Without myself is no great loss to me
For without you there is no life in me.
I'm a madman, desperately holding on
To life as I sink in the blind abyss.
For I'm a man who cannot ever be
Either in you, in God or in myself.
Madam, what can the two of us do now?
For your sweet sake I have abandoned God
Though God himself presented you to me.
I have abandoned God – you are my soul
And I have lost myself, being without you.
I love you. I'm all love. Yet I'm still left
Without myself, without God, without you.

Casandra

God and the Duke. When I consider them
Count, I confess I tremble, for I see
Holy and secular armies arrayed
In an alliance against such a crime.
But, since examples of illicit love
Punctuate every page of history
I feel less guilty. There are precedents.
I'm not inspired by sinners who reformed,
Turning their backs on love, but by those who
Chose love and sin and never turned away.

Count, if there's any remedy for this,
It's this: we must no longer see each other,
We must no longer talk with one another,
So that we'll either die, or love will die,
Now go away from me, for I don't know
If I could ever go away from you.
All that I know is – I would die for you.

Federico

[*Sings*]
I am looking for death
It is all that I have.
I am looking for death
For my soul's in its grave.
So please give me the hand
Which is poisoning me
For I go to the land
Which is death's country.

Casandra   [*Sings*]
                   When I stare in my soul
                   I know this cannot be.
                   Let us listen to God.

Federico   [*Sings*]
                   Let's have no treachery.
                   For you sing with your eyes
                   Like a siren at sea
                   And you lure me to love
                   Where you're murdering me.

Casandra   [*Sings*]
                   Now I fear I'll be lost.

Federico   [*Sings*]
                   And I've no strength to go.

Casandra   [*Sings*]
                   And I cannot resist.

Federico   [*Sings*]
                   And I cannot say no.

Casandra   [*Sings*]
                   And I'm dying for you.

Federico   [*Sings*]
                   My love, so am I.

Casandra   [*Sings*]
                   I am searching for death.

Federico   [*Sings*]
                   Then together we'll die.

Both   [*Sing*]
                   I am looking for death,
                   It is all that I have.
                   I am looking for death,
                   For my soul's in the grave.
                   So please give me the hand
                   Which is poisoning me
                   And we'll go to the land
                   Which is love's country,
                   And we'll go to the land
                   Which is death's country.

Act 3

[*The Duke's Palace*]

[*Enter* AURORA *and* CARLOS]

Aurora   It's true, it's true.

Carlos   I can't believe it.
Be careful, Aurora, lower your voice.

Aurora   Carlos, I only told you this
So I could ask you for advice.

Carlos   How was it possible for you
To observe Federico with the Duchess?

Aurora   I loved the Count and he loved me,
But he was wilier than Ulysses.
With time our love grew strong. It bloomed.
Then he rode off to fetch Casandra.
I expected that we'd be married
When he returned from Mantua.
I trusted all his promises –
How womanly to trust a man!
But when Federico did come home,
He was all melancholy and wan.
The Duke suggested he should be
Married to me, as I'd proposed.
But Federico claimed that he
Had, in my fondness, been replaced
By you. He tried to escape from me
As lovers do, when loving ends,
By feigning jealousy of you
And claiming that you gave him grounds.
Jealousy made as much mark on him
As jealousy makes on a diamond.
Where love does not exist at all
Jealousy cannot touch the mind.
When Federico rejected me
I became stern as steel.
Now jealousy's a sharp-eyed lynx
Can see through a stone wall.
That's how I made my discovery.
There are two arched recesses

In Casandra's dressing room
Covered with looking glasses
Instead of tapestries.
Helped by the many mirrors there
A watching eye may roam
Through a complete reflection of
What seems a second room,
Identical , but then reflected back
Into another mirror, so there seem
A hundred bright receding rooms
And every one the same.
Suspicion cannot be controlled.
Two rooms from them I stood, all ice,
And looked and saw a dreadful sight
In the crystal looking-glass –
His lips, upon her rosy lips,
Delicately alighting.
My soul drained out of me, I ran
Sobbing aloud my mind's misfortune
And the misfortune of two who love
Blindly, while the Duke's away,
So they compete in love and scorn,
Delighting in greater audacity
Than you could find in infidels
Or cannibals, people-eating horrors
Who sea-dogs love to yarn about.
It seemed to me that the mirrors,
Which showed the pair one hundred times,
Darkened their brilliant embrace
As if to hide such a shameless crime.
Then from their lips, their love moved on
To manifold, hundredfold caresses,
And I watched every single one,
Those ventures of sinful kisses.
They say the Duke is riding home,
Laurel-crowned, like a second Mars.
He fought on behalf of the Shepherd of Rome
And scattered all his enemies.
Tell me, Carlos, what can I do?
I'm terrified that you will leave me.
Your words of love, were they really true,
Or, like the Count, will you deceive me?

Carlos   Tell the Duke about our love
               And if he should consent to a

Marriage we will go away
Out of danger to Mantua.
When hunters steal the tiger-cubs,
The tigress, in her agony,
At the loss of her striped children,
Hurls herself into the sea.
So what will brave Ferrara do
For his honour and his good name?
Only bloodshed could remove
Such an ugly, vicious stain,
Unless heaven should intervene
And burn out that stain
By striking both those monsters down
With a thunderstone.
We must leave, that's my advice.

Aurora   Which I accept.

Carlos   This mirror
Shall be like Perseus's shield
Against Medusa's terror.

[*Enter* FEDERICO *and* BATIN]

Federico   Servants went out to meet him on the road.
Why couldn't the Duke wait?

Batin   He left his troops and rode ahead –
And this was for your sake.
He was bursting with impatience
To reach home with all speed,
For love of the Duchess, yes, of course,
But there's no love exceeds
His love for you, Federico,
You're the apple of his eye.
So, Count, prepare a triumph,
For when the Duke's armies come home
To the drums' thunderbeat,
There must be arches overhead
And garlands underfoot.

Federico   Aurora, you always seem to be
Talking with Carlos.

Aurora   What's that to you?

Federico   Is this half-hearted, pale rebuff
Your sole answer to my reproof?

Aurora   Lord, what a wonderful event!
                     Carlos has given you such a slap
                     That even you have felt the sting
                     And woken from four-months' sleep.

Carlos   My lord, I did not know
                     And still don't understand
                     What you are saying now.
                     To you, my noble friend,
                     I would give way in everything
                     Except love. I counted Aurora
                     Safe, as I thought, in the knowledge
                     That I had no rival suitor.
                     You're worthier than me.
                     Though I've not seen you woo her.
                     If that is your true wish
                     Sir, I will leave you to her.

                     [*Exit* CARLOS]

Aurora   What is this plot of yours?
                     What are you thinking of?
                     There's madness in your heart
                     And not a thought of love.
                     How often have you seen
                     Carlos talk with me
                     And by no look or word
                     Have shown your jealousy?
                     And by no look or word
                     Of yours was love implied,
                     But now you turn possessive
                     Since I'm to be a bride.
                     Count, use your intelligence,
                     Let me be a bride.
                     Sooner than help in your pretence
                     I'd commit suicide.
                     Count, revert to your old role –
                     The Melancholy One.
                     My heart remembers all too well
                     The injuries you've done.
                     Count, I can't think about you now.
                     God save me, you deceiver!
                     Too late to use me now that I'm
                     No longer a believer.

                     [*Exit* AURORA]

Batin   By God, what have you done now?

Federico	By God, I swear that I don't know.
Batin	You're like the Emperor Tiberius, who Ordered his wife killed, Sat down at table and shouted to her; "Your supper's getting cold!" And you're also a bit like Messala, The Roman phenomenon. She was the one, you remember, Who forgot her own name.
Federico	I've forgotten that I'm a man.
Batin	Then again, you're a bit like that peasant Who said to his wife with a frown When they'd been married seven years: "Hey look! Your eyes are brown!"
Federico	Oh Batin, I'm in such trouble.
Batin	You're quite like that man from Biscay Who stabled his mule in its bridle And, seeing it wouldn't eat hay, Sent for the local horse doctor Saying: "What is the matter with it?" Whereupon the canny horse doctor Saw the mule's bridle and bit So he sent the mule's owner away, Took the bridle out, chanted a spell So the mule ate a manger of hay And then ate the manger as well. Then back came the man from Biscay Saying: "You've taught him how to chew! From now on my mule and myself Shall be doctored by no-one but you". Let me be your horse doctor, dear Count, Just what are you waiting for? What's this bridle you have in your mouth Which stops you from eating your straw?
Federico	Oh Batin, I don't know what's wrong, But tell me no more anecdotes.
Batin	Well, all right, but don't say anything And don't, for God's sake, touch the oats. [*Enter* CASANDRA *and* LUCRECIA]
Casandra	On his way already?
Lucrecia	Yes madam.

Casandra	So soon?
Lucrecia	To see you, he rode Ahead of his men.
Casandra	Don't believe that story. Oh I'd sooner see My own death. Now, Count, Is the Duke on his way?
Federico	They say he rides fast Out of love for you.
Casandra	I'm dying of grief For what shall we do?
Federico	[*Aside*] His arrival means My love breathes its last.
Casandra	I am losing my senses.
Federico	Mine are long lost.
Casandra	I have lost my soul.
Federico	I have lost my life.
Casandra	What can we do?
Federico	Die.
Casandra	There's no other way?
Federico	No. We are the lost.
Casandra	And must you lose me?
Federico	Oh yes, I must. I must act as a lover I must pretend To be courting Aurora, Ask the Duke for her hand, And this will feed The rumour-hunger Of the palace's Gossip-mongers.
Casandra	Are you insane, Count? Marry her? Why?
Federico	We're both in such danger. There's no other way.
Casandra	What? By God's life If you're cheating me,

You who have caused
This catastrophe,
I'll shout from the housetops –
You don't know me! –
Your wickedness and
My own treachery.

Federico   Madam!

Casandra   Count, there is no more to be said.
The Duke may kill me a hundred times,
But I'll never see you wed.

[*Enter* FEBO, RICARDO *and the* DUKE *in armour*]

Ricardo   The city fathers are still debating
The details of your welcome, sir.

Duke   I owe my speed to passion's spur.

Febo   My mother wouldn't have minded waiting.

Casandra   [*Aside to* FEDERICO]
How can I possibly bear the shame
When you deal with me in this way?

Federico   If you are hurt, then let me say
My love's the only one to blame.

Duke   A father's great love for his son,
Based upon likeness, based upon blood,
Made my journey an easy one.
Neither fatigue nor hardship could
Affect the man whose desire to see
Loved ones brooks no delay. Madam, you should
Please understand that my intense
Love for my son is equalled by
My love for you, and do not take offence.

Casandra   His virtue and his noble birth
Ensure that he deserves your love,
For you are both of equal worth.

Duke   I know that both of you return my love
And both of you deserve more gratitude
Than my tongue can express to you today.
I've heard that Federico's ruled the state
So wisely in my absence that not one
Complaint has been received from any side.
Yes, at the battle's height I thought of him,
Imagining that he would prove himself

A prudent and a perfect overlord.
Thanks be to God, our enemies
Seeing this sword, blessed by the Pope,
Took flight in horror from the slaughterfield.
Later I saw the great Shepherd of Rome
And kissed his hand, then rode through cheering streets
While it rained roses from the Roman roofs.
Because of this, I now intend and swear
To change my wildness into purity,
So that my name, today applauded as
A general's, may one day become a saint's.

Ricardo   Sir, here comes Carlos.

Febo   And Aurora, moreover.

                   [*Enter* CARLOS *and* AURORA]

Aurora   I'm happy to welcome your Highness home.
                   I'm your fervent admirer, as you must know.

Carlos   Give Carlos your hand, sir, I would like
                   To pledge to you my love also.

Duke   Let my embrace repay my heart's deep debts
                   To such a worthy man. Though love dislikes
                   Long partings, all is recompensed
                   When one returns to such displays of love.
                   And now, my dear ones, I would like to rest,
                   And later we will celebrate our joy.

Federico   Heaven preserve you for a hundred years!

                   [*Exeunt all with the* DUKE *except* BATIN, RICARDO *and* FEBO]

Batin   Ricardo the Rhino!

Ricardo   Batin the Bull!

Febo   What about Febo?

Ricardo and Batin
                   Febo the Fool!

Batin   How were the wars?

Ricardo   Once I looked back –
                   The whole plain of Lombardy
                   Is burned black,
                   God fought beside us,
                   Our foes were no trouble,
                   Running like rats

Out of blazing stubble,
But the Lion of the Church –

Febo   – The Duke, that's him –

Ricardo   – With a mighty roar
Tore them limb from limb.
Now Saul slew a thousand,
King David killed more
But one hundred thousand
Was the Duke's score.
Now the Duke of Ferrara's
Bravery
Is resounding throughout
All Italy,
And because of his deeds
In the holy war
The Duke has changed –

Febo   – From what he was before –

Ricardo   – No battles, no bottles,
His wenching is done.
His affection's reserved
For his wife and his son.
Why, the Duke is a saint.

Febo   Yes, he's almost a nun.

Batin   You want me to believe this
Fairy-tale?

Federico   Yes.
Some people, I've heard,
When they've had some success,
Become proud as parrots
And drunkenly stumble
Down the slippery slope –

Ricardo   – But the Duke has turned humble!
He seems not to care
When he's praised by the crowd
For the blood and the banners
Have not made him proud.

Batin   [*Sings*]
There once was a cat,
A black and white cat,
Who longed to be a human.
So hard did she pray

That one fine day
She woke up as a woman.

The woman she sat
Like a sweet ex-cat
When up to her did caper
A mouse and he
Was a poet maybe –
His mouth was stuffed with paper.

Well, her hand went pat!
And the mouse went splat!
The woman purred with laughter.
For a cat's a cat
And a rat's a rat
And they will be ever after.

Ricardo   Don't be afraid
That the Duke will revert
To scrabbling about
In Ferrara's dirt.
For he will have children
Whose soft fingers then
Will comb the great mane
Of this lion among men.

Batin   I'll be very glad
If all this is true.

Ricardo   Goodbye, Batin.

Federico   Yes, farewell to you.

Batin   Where are you going?

Ricardo   I'll just tell you that
It's to see a woman
About a cat.

Febo   I'm going back
For a snooze at my house
Batin – I'm sorry
About the mouse.

[*Exit* RICARDO *and* FEBO. *Enter the* DUKE *with some papers*]

Duke   No servants about?

Batin   I have always been
The Duke's humblest servant –

Duke   – Good Batin!

Batin	God save your highness. Grant that I might Take your hand again.
Duke	What goes on tonight?
Batin	Trust your biography To Ricardo's care, With footnotes by Febo Here and there! I've been hearing their version Of your gallantry. It appears you're the Hector Of Italy.
Duke	While I was away, how did the Count Prove as the guardian of my laws?
Batin	He acquitted himself as well in peace As you have done, sir, in the wars.
Duke	And Casandra, was he kind to her?
Batin	There's never been, as far as I can tell, A step-mother so generously disposed Towards her stepson. Yes, he treats her well. They are as prudent as they're virtuous.
Duke	I'm more grateful than I say That they get on together so admirably, For Federico is the jewel Most estimable and dear to me. I know he was sad when I rode to war To be left behind And so I'm glad Casandra has Been so discreetly kind. I've longed to see these two adopt Loving conciliation. So, here we have two victories, A double celebration. First is the holy victory Which in the wars was won. Second, Casandra's victory In winning her new son. Oh, from this day I'll love her more, And never love another. She's pleased me with her sympathy. My whoring days are over.

| Batin | The Pope has wrought a miracle.
| | A raging, randy drunk
| | Returning from the battlefield
| | Becomes a pious monk.
| | Couldn't you join the Benedictines, sir?
| | They make an excellent liqueur.

Batin
The Pope has wrought a miracle.
A raging, randy drunk
Returning from the battlefield
Becomes a pious monk.
Couldn't you join the Benedictines, sir?
They make an excellent liqueur.

Duke
Let all my citizens be told –
A good Duke's born. The bad Duke's dead.

Batin
The battle, Rome, your journey, sir –
Shouldn't you take a rest in bed?

Duke
As I went up the Palace stairs
Some men approached and they
Gave me some documents to read.
They'd waited there all day.
Such letters often simply beg
But some show wrongs to right.
My conscience says: examine them
Before you sleep tonight.
Batin you may go to bed
But, thanks to my position,
I must, from simple courtesy,
Peruse every petition.

Batin
May heaven reward your conscientiousness,
Prepare her laurels for your victories,
Give guidance for your sure worldly success
And make your name glow down the centuries.

[*Exit* BATIN]

Duke
[*Reading*]
Let's see then: "Sir, I am Estacio,
A labourer in your Palace garden.
I'm good at planting herbs and flowers
And have planted seven children.
The oldest two are budding well,
The younger ones need more nutrition."
I see. I'll be more generous from now on
With rewards for this kind of cultivation.
"Lucinda is the widow of your own
Captain Arnaldo, and she hopes" – I will.
"Albano for the last six years has lived
Without the aid of" – yes, he begs as well.
"Julio was arrested". Same old thing.
"Paula is honoured". Then she lacks nothing.

Now this one's sealed. The man who gave it me
Was dressed in filthy rags. And he was trembling.
"Sir, look closely at your household.
The Count and Duchess are dissembling,
For in your absence −" I'll be calm;
Perhaps they governed inefficiently.
"They stained your honour and your bed
With infamous audacity."
Can I contain the anger which
Rises at this catastrophe?
"Be discreet and your eyes shall show
That which your heart least wants to know."
What are these words?
Words, answer me!
Are you liars?
How could this be?
I'm the father
Of this son.
Has he robbed me?
What has he done?
No, you're liars.
Don't you realise
They couldn't deceive me!
But the paper replies:
To betray is easy −
Anyone can.
She is a woman.
He is a man.
Small cruel words
To say I should know
There is nowhere that people
Dare not go.
God summed up my sins −
This is how I must pay.
Nathan cursed David
In the same way.
And I shall grieve
As David has done.
O Federico,
My son, my son.
Yet a greater penalty
Seems to be mine.
Casandra's my wife.
Not a concubine

Like David's Bathsheba.
Uriah's wife.
But I haven't taken
Uriah's life.
My traitor, my son!
But, is it true?
I don't believe
A man's son could do
Such a terrible thing.
I'll kill you and then
I will engender you again
And then I will kill you
All over again
And then I'll engender —
What treachery when
All's said and done!
A father can't leave his house,
Trusting his son.
But how can I find out
What has gone on
Without witnesses knowing
My honour has gone?
Questions won't help
For who'd dare tell me
The true facts about
Such disloyalty?
I don't need evidence
Tell me who
Would allege such a thing
Unless it were true?
To punish these two
Is not taking revenge.
Do executioners
Take revenge?
And I need no proof.
No-one needs to commit
Such a vicious deed
If men speak of it.
If they have ruined
My good name
By deed or by rumour —
It's all the same.

[*Enter* FEDERICO]

Federico	They say you will not rest And so I came. I wanted To ask a favour of you.
Duke	God save you. It is granted.
Federico	You announced your hope – that Aurora and I Should be married in your palace. But I was filled with jealousy Over the Marquis Carlos. That's why I disobeyed you sir. But, ever since you went, My love has grown, my jealousy Seems insignificant. And so we made peace – Aurora and I – And I told her of my decision: That we should be married as soon as you Can grant us your permission. This, sir, is what I ask for now.
Duke	You could not give me greater pleasure. Count, this is very good to know. Go and discuss this with your mother For we must listen to her voice. It is not right for you to marry Without deferring to her views, Just as you asked for my consent.
Federico	Considering that I'm not of her blood, Surely, father, you see I can't Ask her about this. I don't think I should.
Duke	What does blood matter to you? Casandra is your mother now.
Federico	My mother was Laurencia. She has lain in her grave for many a year.
Duke	Do you object to calling her "mother"? I've been told that, when I was away, You got on very well together.
Federico	As to that, God only knows, And I don't want to complain, Since you adore her, and rightly so. She is an angel to everyone, But not to me, sir, not to me.
Duke	I've been misled, for I was told You delighted Casandra more Than anyone in the world.

Federico	Well, sometimes she is kind to me.
	At others she says: A man who's born
	To one woman cannot ever be
	Another woman's actual son.
Duke	That's obvious, and I agree.
	However, I'd be better pleased
	If she'd loved you rather than me
	So she might have kept the peace.
	So, go with God.

[*Exit* FEDERICO]

Treacherous Count, how could I look
Into your infamous face?
So you've made it up with Aurora?
What a liar! What a disgrace!
The thing that really convinces me
Is how careful he was to say
That Casandra treated him badly
While I was away.
Wickedness thinks it hides every trace
When its crime is as plain as the nose on a face.
He avoids calling her mother –
I don't blame him.
Call his mistress "mother" in bed?
That might shame even him.
But how can I so readily bring
Myself to believe this terrible thing?
Perhaps the story's invented?
The Count has an enemy
Out for revenge, who knows how
I'd punish such treachery.
Yes, oh yes, this must be the case.
I was wrong to believe. That is my disgrace.

[*Enter* AURORA *and* CASANDRA]

Aurora	I trust that you, my lady,
	Will help on this occasion.
Casandra	Aurora, you have made
	A very wise decision.
Aurora	Here is the Duke.
Casandra	Oh, sir,
	Are you not resting yet?
Duke	No – in my absence there
	Arose affairs of state

	Which I must grapple with right now.
	This letter proves that you
	And Federico too
	Ruled well, and you should know
	The writer pleads you both should have
	Everything which you deserve.
Casandra	To the Count, sir, not to me
	You owe these words of warmth.
	I say, without flattery,
	He has heroic worth.
	He is superior in all his deeds
	And he's as brave as he's discreet.
	Yes, sir, he has been the image of you.
Duke	The image of me in everything . . . ..
	I know he has been my substitute
	And you have taken him for me.
	For which, madam, I'm promising,
	You'll be rewarded suitably.
Casandra	I bring one more petition, sir,
	It's easy to despatch.
	Carlos and Aurora –
	Do you approve their match?
Duke	I think she has the one she loves
	Most in all the land.
	The Count just left me and he asked
	For Aurora's hand.
Casandra	The Count asked for Aurora?
Duke	Yes he did. Casandra.
Casandra	The Count?
Duke	Yes.
Casandra	Is it true?
Duke	They will be married tomorrow.
Casandra	Then let them do what they want to do.
Aurora	Forgive me, your highness.
	I don't want the Count.
Duke	What next? A rebellion?
	Aurora, you can't
	Suggest that Carlos
	Competes with the Count
	In courage or lineage.

Aurora	Perhaps I can't.
	[*Sings*] When I loved him the other day The young man turned me down, sir. Now that he wants me, it's fair play The other way around, sir.
Duke	Do it for me, not for him, sweet maid.
Aurora	I've lost my taste for the Count, I'm afraid.
	[*Exit* AURORA]
Duke	A determined lady.
Casandra	Aurora is right Though she answers too boldly.
Duke	No, she is not. Aurora shall marry him, Like it or not.
Casandra	Sir, love is always A matter of taste. Love is a flower That cannot be forced.
	[*Exit the* DUKE]
	That treacherous Count! Throwing my love away!
	[*Enter* FEDERICO]
Federico	Was my father not here?
Casandra	Oh, such infamous calm! So you'll marry Aurora? Hide you face, traitor.
Federico	Hide your love, lady, Consider our danger.
Casandra	Our danger, you villain? I'm too angry to care.
Federico	Lower your voice Or the whole world will hear.
	[*Enter the* DUKE, *concealing himself*]
Duke	I'm trying to prove If they are in love. But I can't stand the thought Of what I'll find out.

Federico	Listen lady, try to preserve Your dignity, if nothing else.
Casandra	What other man in the whole world Would abandon me like this? It is simple cowardice. You said love would last When you broke down my resistance With your sighs and your persistance. You took my love. What do I get?
Federico	Madam, I'm not married yet. I aim to reassure the Duke And save our lives, pray God. But even with amazing luck Our love can't come to good. For the Duke's not just any man And it would drive him mad If his honourable name Were trampled in the mud. Love made us blind. That time of love must end.
Casandra	Bastard – Look at my tears. Coward – I've no more fear. I can feel no more hurt For a dog ate my heart.
Duke	If I stay, I'll turn to stone. Unhappy man, what did you expect? They have confessed without the rack. Oh no – for I was on the rack. Now I need no more coins of proof, I have the full amount. Honour, you be the judge Of their punishment. But it must not reflect Upon my own good name. Such things performed in public Mar a great man's fame. No human being must know What my dishonour is. I must conceal that stain As if it never was. For though a just act seems

To wipe out an insult,
That insult lives if everyone
Discovers the foul fault.

[*Exit* DUKE]

Casandra   Women are chained to bad luck.
Men are made out of fraud.

Federico   Madam, I'll do whatever you wish,
I give you my word.

Casandra   Is that really true?

Federico   Infallible.

Casandra   Then everything is possible.
Once I was yours, I am yours again.
We must see each other every day.

Federico   Go now, my lady
And, since you are discreet,
Pretend that you enjoy yourself
With the Duke tonight.

Casandra   Without being false to you, sweetheart,
I will go to the Duke and I'll play that part.

[*Exeunt* FEDERICO *and* CASANDRA. *Enter* AURORA *and* BATIN]

Batin   They tell me you're getting married
To the Marquis Carlos and mean
Shortly to move to Mantua –
Would you mind taking Batin?

Aurora   Batin, I'm surprised that you want to go
And leave Ferrara and Federico.

Batin   Working a lot and making a little
Is the sort of insult that can
Either kill or drive crazy
The sanest, wisest man.
Today "Yes, of course". Tomorrow: "No".
"Maybe", "Another time", "Come here", "Please go".
I don't know what or who is up
But I do know that I don't want to know.
Apart from all this, the Count's bewitched.
He changes every minute, rude, then kind,
Sad as a saucepan, merry as a monkey.
Hello, I'm sane! Goodbye – out of my mind.
Then take the Duchess, no, you take her –

Insufferable is what she's been.
When it's going badly for everyone else
How can it go well for Batin?
The Duke's become a phoney saint –
Talks to himself the whole day through.
Oh, the whole household's a dead loss.
I'll come to Mantua with you.

Aurora   If the Duke gives me to Carlos
You shall come along with me.

Batin   God bless you, God bless the Marquis.
I'll go and tell him immediately.

[*Exit* BATIN. *Enter the* DUKE]

Duke   Honour, my fierce enemy!
Who invented your cruel maze?
A twisted genius, half-crazed,
Bent on revenge for some atrocity?
For his system has always meant
Dishonour falls on the most innocent.
Aurora!

Aurora   Sir!

Duke   The course of action
Recommended by the Duchess
Is that you should marry Carlos,
And I'd rather grant her satisfaction
Than please the Count.

Aurora   My thanks indeed.

Duke   Tell Carlos to write to Mantua now.

Aurora   I will run and tell him how
Generously you've agreed.

[*Exit* AURORA]

Duke   Heaven, your punishment alone
Shall be done in my domain.
Raise your great rod. Let it come down.
It's not revenge for the wrong that's done
For I have no vengeful intent.
Revenge is yours, for it's obscene
For father to wreak vengeance on his son.
This must be heaven's punishment.
A punishment without revenge shall soon
Fall on the shameless doers of this sin.

I shall be merely heaven's instrument.
This is what the laws of honour
Say: that there must never be
Public knowledge of my injury
For that would double my dishonour.
To punish your foe in the public square
Is to double your honour's hurt,
Not only do you lose your good name, but
You spread the bad news everywhere.

I've put Casandra in a chair nearby,
Trussed hand and foot and waist and neck
And covered her with a silk sack
And, so that nobody will hear her cry,
I gagged her. So she waits in her coccoon.
She was simplicity to bind
For, after I briefly explained,
She made things easy with a swoon.
Such traps await all who betray.
It serves them right. But, oh my Lord,
To put one's dear son to the sword –
I think of it, I faint away.
My soul feels the ice-touch of death.
My body trembles. Tears in my eyes.
In my cold veins the bloodstream dies.
My breast heaves and cannot draw breath.
My memory is a seething mob of crime.
My will to action is boiling up
Like a stream that's been dammed up
By the snows of wintertime.

I'll judge him with love. Now I understand.
God says honour thy father.
God says honour thy mother.
The Count has broken each command.
I must punish him lovingly.
With contempt he treated his own father
And, if today he takes my honour,
Tomorrow he may take my life from me.

Ataxerxes had less cause than me
When he cut down fifty men.
Brutus took justice without revenge
And his knife spoke most eloquently.
No, my love cannot erase
My right to deal out punishment.
Honour, this great court's president,

Wants to pass judgement on the case.
The public prosecutor, truth,
Has laid the charge. Guilty! It's clear,
Witnessed by the eye and ear
Which swore, in God's name, to the proof.

The lawyers, love and blood, would seem
To form a very strong defence.
But guilt and shame and rank offence
Are on the prosecution team.
God is the judge by whom my son is tried.
Here he comes. Heaven be at my side.

[*Enter* FEDERICO]

Federico   Aurora and the Marquis, sir –
I'm told they'll marry, then to Mantua,
And this with your permission, sir?

Duke   Count, gossip flies on wayward wings.
I gave no consent to Carlos and Aurora.
My mind's been busy with higher things.

Federico   There's little rest for a ruler of men.
What is worrying you, sir?

Duke   Son, one of our noblemen
Has hatched a conspiracy
But he placed his trust in a woman
Who revealed the secret to me.
Only a fool trusts a woman.
A wise man makes use of this fact.
I summoned the traitor by saying
I had a business to transact.
Once alone I said: "So you'd kill me?"
He fainted, then and there.
When he woke up he was bound hand and foot,
Gagged and tied to a chair.
I've covered him up with a silken sack
So whoever takes his life
Won't know who he is, thus avoiding
A vendetta and civil strife.
Since you are here, act for me,
Be my executioner.
Resolutely drew your sword
And kill me a traitor, sir.
From here I'll watch how zealously
You dispatch my enemy.

Federico	Are you, by any chance, testing me, Or was this a genuine conspiracy?
Duke	When his father orders his son to do Anything, should he ask why? Get out with your wheres and whyfores, Go away, coward, and I . . . ..
Federico	Put up your sword. Wait here, sir. I'm not scared, for I know This person is bound and gagged. But My heart shakes, even so.
Duke	Let me do it, coward.
Federico	I'm going. Your order's enough for me. sir. Oh, but heavens above.
Duke	A coward? A rat?
Federico	I go my lord, if it were Caesar himself I would give him For you, one thousand blows.

[*Exit* FEDERICO, *his sword drawn*]

Duke	I can see him from here. There he goes. The point goes through her and through her. The man who dishonoured me Is executing my justice. Guards! Servants! Somebody! Quick!

[*Enter* CARLOS, AURORA, BATIN, RICARDO, FEBO *and all others*]

      The Count has killed Casandra
 Because she, his stepmother,
 Told him she had a better son
 In her womb, another
 Who must succeed me. Kill him!

Carlos	The Count?
Duke	Murdered my wife!
Carlos	I shall not leave for Mantua Until I take his life.
Duke	Here comes the traitor Stained with his disgrace.

[*Enter* FEDERICO *with his sword drawn and bloody*]

Federico	I killed your traitor for you, Then I uncovered the face And found –
Duke	– No more words! Silence! Kill him! Kill him!
Carlos	[*Striking* FEDERICO] Die!
Federico	Oh father, why are you having me killed?

[*Pursued by* CARLOS, *he dies behind the curtain*]

Duke	In God's court they'll tell you why. Aurora, leave with Carlos. He is worthy in every way.
Aurora	I am, sir, so confused that I Do not know what to say.
Batin	Say yes, there are good reasons For all you see, Aurora.
Aurora	Your highness, by tomorrow You shall have my answer.

[*Re-enter* CARLOS]

Carlos	The Count is dead.
Duke	My eyes are straining not to cry. At the same time they long to look upon The body of the man who was my son.

[DUKE *draws back curtain to show the bodies of* FEDERICO *and* CASANDRA]

Carlos	The Duke views his son's corpse without spite, For justice was done, it served him right.
Duke	Here I stand, but my courage fails. Let my tears fall as bright as nails. All this – to gain an inheritance. All this – and that is all, dear audience.
Batin	Lost in a mirror, that's their tragedy And you may think it serves them right. This was a scandal throughout Italy And an example to us all tonight.

[*The End*]